Ethical Theft
How to
Steal Business
From Your Competition

by Don Farrell

Don Farrell
Visit his website at www.FreshRevenues.com
Printed in the United States of America

Third Printing: July, 2011

ISBN 978-0-9825497-0-4

Table of Contents

INTRODUCTION

Does the World Need Another Book?

It has been said that all human accomplishments that are not motivated by love are, in the end, empty. If you are motivated by the idea that you can and should provide for others—those you love, then **YES!**, you need this book. And may you love like you've never loved before.

This book will teach you how to steal business from your competition. Why? There is only so much business to be had. Your competition has business you need in order to provide for those you love. You might ask, "Well, doesn't my competition deserve to provide for those they care about too?" The short answer: No, they don't. Is this ethical, un-ethical, moral, or immoral, and how far are you willing to go? Better yet, how far does your employer expect you to go in order to provide? Do his or her scruples align with your personal principles and standards? Who is right and who is wrong? If you have been asking these same questions, then **YES!**, you need to read this book.

These are the issues I deal with in this book. I offer tactical steps and stories on the stuff that I did while working in the sales offices of hotels and while running the world's largest sales and service training company.

If you are reading this book and are not in the hotel business, **YES!**, you still need this book. I think you will see parallels or similarities between what we do in the world of hospitality and what can be done in your world.

This book was born out of experience. Starting as a hotel pot scrubber at age 15 and working my way up through the ranks, I wound up in the sales arena. At my current age of 52, I have taken my best tactics and my best stories, and have assembled them for you to learn and execute. If you don't use them to sell, then **YES!**, you need this book in order to know what to do to prevent others from stealing business from you.

After reading this book, I would love to hear your thoughts and recommendations on how to make it better. I would especially like to hear your own business liberating stories in hopes that I get enough of them to produce a follow-up book. If you would like, I will include your contact information in the new book. Please e-mail me at Don@FreshRevenues.com.

Dedication

In the summer of 1971, a want ad looking for a maître d' at a swanky Marriott hotel caught my eye. Even by the age of 16, I had already logged a few years of mopping floors, stocking bars, cutting the grass, washing dishes, and bussing tables. So in my not-so-humble opinion, I was ready to move up in the world. I was ready to know what a maître d' was and ready for whatever he did.

I drove to the hotel and went to the front desk to find out where I needed to go. Standing behind the 5-foot desk is a 4-foot 11-inch gal who listened to what I had to say. She then escorted me into the kitchen. I had no idea at the time that Mary Martin, as it turned out, worked in accounting and was not normally at the front desk. She was doing something they almost never did with job applicants. Under regular circumstances this hotel had job applicants fill out basic paperwork and then send them home to wait for a 'yes-we-need-you/no-we-don't' call. So I figured this maître d' gig must have been as big a deal as I imagined, or maybe, I thought, Mary was grasping the overwhelming presence of my years of experience to do the job.

So off we went ... to the kitchen ... Mary in the lead and me following quickly behind in my best reversible JCPenney polyester suit. If you're of my generation, you know this versatile statement of high fashion. Two color options: one light for casual summer wear and one dark for winter and/or funerals. My suit was brown on one side and, this day, I wore the ivory side out. I think Mary noticed my practical side thanks to that classy suit.

Mary and I eventually came upon three gentlemen crammed into a closet-sized office just off the prep area of the kitchen. Then she left me with a wink and one last wish of good luck. I was pretty sure I needed little luck to land this job. Afterall, I had skills!

All three managers had their backs turned to me while they were reviewing some blueprints. I interrupted them with my announcement that I had come to take that maître d' position. One of the men turned to look at me with his "Clint Eastwood as Dirty Harry" squinty-eyes. After about five seconds of silence with all three men just standing there staring at me, Dirty Harry started berating me—questioning why I had ever thought I could do the job of maître d'. Further insults revolved around the fact that I didn't even know what a maître d' was and how I was wasting precious seconds of their time. I lost track of whatever else he said because all I wanted to do at this point was find the closest exit.

I won't say I started to cry, but I was having some difficulty seeing my way to the closest exit. My departure was undoubtedly going to be less pompous and grand than my arrival. Heck, I would have jumped through a hole in the wall if one had existed.

As I was jetting to freedom, an arm grabbed me from behind and spun me around. I turned to face another of the three managers. His name was Scott Huth and he asked if I wanted a different job in his hotel. I'm not sure what he saw in me other than my guts and blind confidence, but he offered and I nodded yes.

He told me to show up the next day, and that he'd put me to work. That's the day I began my 30+ years in the hotel business —as a pot scrubber.

So to the Mary Martins and the Scott Huths of the world, this book is dedicated to you and the passion you bring to all aspiring maître d's. ■

How To Use This Book

Stealing business is not just about knowing how to acquire the intel about which clients are working with your competitors. I want you to know how to make a sales call that will be worthy of earning a potential client's trust and loyalty. Trust and loyalty are words you see a lot in this book. They look strange right next to the words stealing and liberating, but it will hopefully make more sense as you read on.

This book is structured to help you go into the world and do the following:

- Develop the right frame of mind to channel the passion you have to provide and produce good things.

- Have access to all the skill sets needed to make the very best sales calls.

- Find out which of the more than 50 business-stealing approaches shared in this book work best for you in liberating clients from your competition.

  I know that I use a lot of hotel referencing in here, but use these stories to get your creative juices going and consider how many of these tactics will work in your business.

- "Steal" the business before your competition even knows that the business is out there.

  Picture this invisible wave of business floating around in the world. The business is going to land somewhere. Whether it lands with you or with your competitors remains to be seen. Go get some before they do.

Frame of Reference

I think it is important for you, the reader, to know what possessed or motivated the author of this book (or any book in which you have invested good money). What is his or her intent and what gives that person credibility. Why should you believe and act upon the stuff that he or she shares?

I have no aspirations of being just a writer. Writing for me is a conduit into the speaking world. I figure, if I can speak to you and you read this book (or vice-versa), there's a better chance that you will actually change your life for the better. Ultimately, I am hoping that after people hire me to speak to their groups that I will then get to really partner with them on some initiative(s) that can truly make a difference—a difference for them, their clients, their employees, their brand, their lenders, their community, and oh yeah, me. Simply put, the end game for me is to work with people who are as passionate as I am about doing good work for good people.

The following jobs, experiences, and situations are my frame of reference—what shaped my thinking and made me enough of an expert to write a book. Rest assured, I didn't want to model myself after every boss I had, but I always looked for the good in each of them. Better yet, I got to see and experience firsthand the mistakes my bosses made resulting from poor business decisions. This is the stuff you can't learn in books.

My 30 previous jobs (to date):

- Made Italian ice and pulled weeds for the neighbors as a kid growing up in Brooklyn, New York.

- Washed dishes at age 15 for the Clifford Supper Club in Wisconsin.

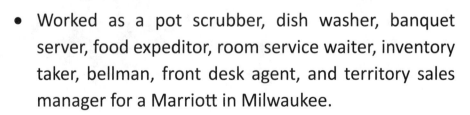

- Held such positions as floor mopper, bar stocker, grass cutter, bus boy, fence painter, banquet set-up, and caterer to outside companies while with the Linden Terrace Supper Club in Wisconsin.

- Worked as a pot scrubber, dish washer, banquet server, food expeditor, room service waiter, inventory taker, bellman, front desk agent, and territory sales manager for a Marriott in Milwaukee.

- Secured corporate business from two states for 10 hotels while working as a regional sales manager at Holiday Inns Inc. based in Minneapolis.

- Brought business into four of the *best* Holiday Inns in the world while working as sales manager in Chicago.

- Directed sales for Holiday Inn Oak Brook Terrace in Chicago.

- Served as the food and beverage director for the Holiday Inn Oak Brook Terrace.

- Worked as the pre-opening director of sales for a brand new Holiday Inn in Detroit.

- Was the director of sales at a company-owned Holiday Inn in St. Louis that had the greatest net operating profit in the region.

- Managed regional sales at 40 company-owned hotels based in D.C.

- Promoted seven pretty terrific Sheraton resorts and conference centers in the northeast while working as vice president of marketing for Inn America Hotels.

- Oversaw revenues at more than 30 Holiday Inns while vice president of sales for Flautt Properties.

- Founded and was chairman of Signature Worldwide (www.signatureworldwide.com), which eventually became not only the best sales and service training company in the world, but the largest with 265 employees and licensees in 44 countries.

- Started entreprenYour inc. and then became Founder and Chief Cultivator at Fresh Revenues (www.FreshRevenues.com). ■

Chapter I: Ethical Theft

The initial title of this book had nothing to do with the question of ethics. My original intent was to take 50 of my best tactical stealing stories and combine them with another 50 from other professionals who had stories that could add to your thieving repertoire. So, I plugged into a lot of blogs that attracted a lot of salespeople, asking them to share their best story or two. My plan was to then fly out and interview the best contributors to validate their claims in exchange for a mention in this book. Instead of getting these great stories, I was getting comments like, "We should not be stealing from one another. We should be helping each other" or "I don't think stealing is a good word. You should tone it down some." I also heard a slew of stories from salespeople who thought stealing from their competition was just the same as acquiring business because the client walked into their office and the salesperson was nice to the buyer.

I did have one fascinating exchange with a gentleman who specializes in corporate espionage. He was telling me about foreign companies that invest millions in eavesdropping equipment. They point their parabolic dishes and other high-tech equipment at research and development buildings here in the United States to pirate technology before it comes to market. It sounded like something out of a James Bond movie, and I have no doubt he was telling the truth, as he cautioned me to tread lightly with stories of stealing business.

I wanted a book that contains tactical stories that the average salesperson could use when selling anything from hotel rooms to computer software. Needless to say, I was finding much of the information I was gathering to be useless.

I then questioned why my perspective on stealing from the competition was so different from the majority? I started making calls to fellow salespeople from my past in order to get their input. A few of them had some good stuff that I have included in the book. Others admitted to past practices of liberating business that they were now ashamed to admit. After getting them to tell me about these things off the record, I found 90 percent of what they did in the past to be perfectly legitimate. Evidently, my moral compass must be pointing in a different direction from most other people. I realized that until we all agreed what was fair, unfair, right, wrong, ethical or unethical, I was going to have a harder time than I imagined getting you to be more committed to taking what is rightfully yours. That is when it became clear to me that I needed to first define what was ethical, what was not, and how far each of us is willing to go in the never-ending quest to increase revenues.

eth-ic [eth-ik], *n.* a system of moral standards.

eth-i-cal [eth-i-k*uh*l], *adj.* conforming to professional standards of conduct.

What becomes clear is that we all have our own ideas of what is moral; what professional means; and certainly what defines a standard of conduct. So, I picked up the phone and started calling many of my colleagues to help me define "ethical." Many had trouble with the definition and one gentleman even told me that he has never done a single unethical thing in his life. I know this guy, so it took me about 30 seconds of questioning him on specific selling tactics, in which he had

WEBSTER : ETH*IC, A SYSTEM OF MORAL STANDARDS,ETH*I*CAL, CONFORMING TO PROFESSIONAL STANDARDS OF CONDUCT, engaged, before he admitted that he may not be as pure as the driven snow. After conducting this phone blitz, I don't think I got any closer to a uniform definition of what is ethical and what is not. The one thing that was clear is that folks either had not given it much thought or they had very different interpretations from one to the next.

I don't know if I can define ethical as well as I can define unethical, so I offer you my heart-felt definition

in the following pages. You are or will be in a situation where others are relying on you to provide for them. Your wife, husband, kids, grandparents, brothers, sisters, and even friends depend on you. Picture them now. If you don't bring home the money, they suffer to some degree. It could be a situation where they won't be able to buy a car they need to get a job. It could be monies needed for a college education, or it could be something as simple as being able to buy Christmas or Hanukah gifts. These are the folks you love, and they love you. They probably won't love you any less if you don't provide for them, but they are still counting on you to provide none the less.

Let's go beyond those you define as people you "love," and think about people you like and need. Using a hotel example, let's say you have 50 employees working in the building—housekeeping, maintenance, front desk, food servers and so on. Those employees have 2.3 family members on the average. These people are relying on YOU to provide the revenues needed to make your business successful so that their loved ones can continue to work at the hotel.

Now we have the vendors or purveyors who provide goods and services to this hotel who may be counting on this account for the things they need, including a job. They too have 2.3 family members to support. So if we add up the amount of people counting on YOU to drive revenues, the number escalates from 50 employees to somewhere around 150 people.

If you think you live paycheck to paycheck, I would suggest that you walk in the shoes of someone making minimum wage or even close to it. This concept really hit home for me when I was working as the director of sales for a hotel sales department that delivered about 80 percent of the hotel's revenues—an unusually high number and something of which we were fiercely proud. We were confident, but I also felt we were getting too cocky.

The Christmas and Hanukah holiday season was approaching, and as often happens in the hotel business, we were slowing down. I asked the head housekeeper what she was going to have to do with her minimum wage employees. She told me she would have to lay them off for more than three weeks because we did not have enough business to justify the extra payroll. To get our cocky back to confident, I told her that we, the sales staff, would tell these employees about the layoff. So, my normally proud and confident sales force that had made hundreds of sales presentations to some pretty tough audiences in the past, made quite a shaky showing when they gave their "you can't come to work  for three weeks because we don't have enough business" presentation to our housekeeping staff.

The reaction of those minimum wage employees was quite remarkable. They offered to work for less pay. They offered to work two days and get paid just one. They asked us if there was anything they could do to make a little extra money, so that they could afford to buy their families gifts for the holidays and pay for the gas needed to visit relatives. Despite the tears, the despair, and the borderline begging for work, we had to tell them no. That sales staff—*my sales staff*— went back to their work with a fresh perspective on who and how many people were counting on them to deliver. They saw and felt the hurt firsthand, and darn it if they did not find some business the week after Christmas to put a few of those who were going to be laid off back to work.

That was an experience I will never ever forget, and if you ever need an injection to get your passion and focus going again, I suggest you really get to know some of your employees who live paycheck to paycheck.

So back to the question of what is ethical and unethical when it comes to selling and stealing business from the competition. My definition of unethical is this: Failing to do anything and everything within my power, and without breaking the law, to provide for my loved ones, my employees, and my employees' families.

I don't lie, I don't cheat, and I care about my co-workers. I try hard to be one of the most ethical people I know, but I will definitely steal business from my competition, and I am more than OK with that.

Now if you say, "The competition has employees and families too," I say, "If I can steal their business, then they don't deserve it." If I can take their business from

them, those clients and customers were not as happy as they deserved to be, and therefore not as loyal as they should have been. Why not? It's my job to find out and deliver in a way that makes them loyal to me, or someone will steal them from me someday. The same goes for your employees too. If I try to steal an account from a competitor and that account will not move, then I need to find another account or different competitor to pursue. It is very difficult or even impossible to steal business and employees from a competitor who does a great job.

I worked as a vice president of sales for a hotel management company and when a competitor was able to take one of our hotel managers from us (which happened a lot), the powers that be would get violently upset—at the wrong person. They would blame the competition for stealing our help, when they should be blaming themselves.

That, my friends, is an ego run amok. They should have been asking themselves why they were losing such good people and then taken serious and genuine steps to fix their culture. As it was, they did nothing and the company is no more.

Imagine a world, which we could live in today, where corporations were driving every minute of every day to make their clients and their employees so happy that loyalty would never be an issue. Nobody could come along and steal employees from you because every employee would always feel the passion you have for them and their families.

Can you imagine how much better service in America would be if we would get that serious and focused about caring for our people?

This brings us to the idea that stealing business can take a company to a higher plane—one that involves an organization's culture. Businesses today are looking for a competitive edge wherever and whenever they can get it. They are spending absolute fortunes on developing competitive edges that, in all too many cases, are temporary because competitors copy products or services, or get into a short-sighted race trying to one-up each other. These kinds of edges, in my opinion, are commodities. Anything short of a competitive edge involving company culture is only a temporary fix. What all organizations should be aspiring to have is a culture built on a sales and service cornerstone—one in which management is committed to making employees and clients as loyal as humanly possible. Now that is something your competition cannot easily replicate if you have the passion to execute.

To conclude this chapter, I would like to share one bloggers definition of ethical. He said, "If you are willing to go on the evening news, while your family is watching, and tell the world what you did with a good conscience, then it is ethical."

What Business Are We Talking About?

For simplicity's sake, there are two kinds of selling situations—transactional selling and relationship selling.

Transactional selling is the type of selling where you are answering phones, answering incoming e-mails, or working at a counter and someone inquires about your product or service. Typically, you don't have a lot of time to spend on this potential buyer because you are motivated to move quickly and wait on the next person in line. Transactional selling is the kind of call you would make to the cable company, or when you stand in line at AutoZone (I have had some personal experiences here so I hope this company calls me at 901-853-4885).

Pick a number from 1-10, with 10 being the best service experience you could possibly imagine, and rate the service provided by the cable company or AutoZone. Don't pick based on the service you want, but what you think you would get. Why didn't you say a nine or 10? I know why. It's because you are not used to getting that level of service. Why don't you get that kind of service? Here are a few reasons:

- Too many companies incorrectly see transactional selling as an operations function—almost like working in a factory assembly line. Answer the potential customer's question; give him or her a canned and scripted message; and be conscious of your talk time. Time on the phone costs money and customers don't like to wait in lines that are very long. Employees often have a "get 'em in and get 'em out" mentality. Ask any of these companies what their call or walk-in conversion rate is (the number of inquiries compared to the number of people who actually buy), and they won't be able to tell you. This is a service and selling opportunity that needs to be treated with the same passion that you have for your employees and your current customers. I will share a formula with you later in this chapter on how to create loyalty.

- Too many employees doing these jobs can't visualize where their current job can take them. They don't realize that they are learning skills (or should be) that will make them better at whatever it is they want to do.

- Employers don't care enough about why employees are working at their company. If they knew more about their employees' wants and needs, they could explain to employees how the job could help them realize their ultimate goal. The employer would also structure training to compliment the job and the individual's passions.

Here is an example. You hire a 19-year-old to work at your hotel's front desk or at your hardware store's counter. He is majoring in criminal justice. You find out through the interviewing process that he wants to be a police officer in a big city—not your little town. You ask him what skills he would need to not just be a police officer, but to be an elite, best-of-the-best police officer. He probably has never been asked that question before, so it takes a while to get an answer.

"Well, I will need to learn how to shoot a gun," he says. You say, "Hopefully you won't need that skill in this job, so it will be hard for me to teach you that skill. What other skills do you need?" He goes through a few before hitting on some with which you can help. You know there is a very important skill that isn't mentioned, so you ask, "Have you thought about the training you will need to stay calm and productive while under great pressure?" You make it clear that this is something of real value which he can and will learn in this job. You are committing to making him not only the best in this particular role while working for you, but the best in whatever role he holds in the future. You will discuss monthly how much closer he is coming to realizing his dream as a police officer. Each month, as you conclude your informal chat on progress made, you share something that you are doing to help him. One month, you find a book on detective work that you think he would enjoy. The next month, you give him the phone number and name of a policeman you talked to on his behalf who is willing to have a cup of coffee with your employee and talk about police work. The list goes on.

Think about the things you can do to express how much you care about each employee—one by one. If you have a lot of employees, then their immediate supervisors need to fill this role. You may only have this employee for three more years. Heck, you may only have them for a year, but it will be one terrific year where your sales and service culture drives you to being the best.

- Employees are not trained correctly. Most training fails because it is not reinforced properly. That was how the company I founded and ran until June of 2007 became the best and the biggest sales and service training company in the world. We knew how to make the skill sets we taught work in spite of turnover.

- You hired the wrong employee. This individual might have been a good employee in a different job function, but not in the one that required him or her to service and sell.

So, let's say you hired the right person. You need to discover her personal and professional goals and orient her to your culture. Then you should train and reinforce the skill sets you want her to have. If it is sales and service skills you are looking for to drive maximum sales conversions, consider the eight-step transactional formula.

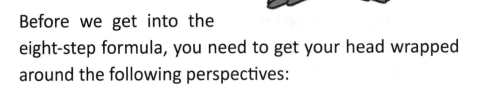

Before we get into the eight-step formula, you need to get your head wrapped around the following perspectives:

Be customer centric. Focus on what is important to the buyer. Make it easy for them to do business with you instead of just trying to make it easier for you. Think about how upset you get when you hear, "That's our company policy" from a service provider or you encounter an employee who is unable or unwilling to be helpful.

Create the best value proposition. Most buyers are not looking for the best price, but are instead looking for the best value. They may start the conversation with "What is the cheapest price?" but often change their view. Think about the number of times you went into a store to buy something and you anticipated spending a certain dollar amount. You got to the store, and you saw that there was a slightly more expensive option that had a few more benefits with greater value. The reason we all spend more than we intended to spend is because we get a lot more value for a little bit of money. Even minimum wage employees make these kinds of value proposition buying decisions. Value proposition selling in a transactional selling situation is a smart way to go.

Be a consultant. I learned a long time ago that consumers don't like to be sold, but they do love to buy. Think again about the times that someone pressed you into buying something. You may have bought it but you will never go back to that business. Do not pressure anyone into buying your product or service. Instead, make it easy for them by communicating real value. This comes from first understanding what the customer needs. The Golden Rule says to do unto others as you would have them do unto you. The Platinum Rule, created by prolific author and behavioral style assessment expert Dr. Tony Alessandra, says to treat others as they want to be treated, meaning you need to find out what is important to the potential buyer.

Don't overwhelm the buyer. Offer just a few options and make it a conversation — not a script. As consumers, we like options but not a confusing amount. We want just a few from which to choose.

Care about the customer. Do not worry about how the buyers will pay until you have determined their needs, created value, offered options, and quoted pricing. Once they say yes, then you get into payment methods. A hotel accounting person once told me, "We need to get buyers to fall in love with us before we ever begin to think about how they will pay." I wish more salespeople knew and practiced that mantra.

Educate the prospective buyer. Anytime someone calls you, e-mails you or visits your business, teach them something new about your product or service. Perhaps you can mention a new benefit, an update, or even a story someone told you about how they used your product.

With this new mind shift to transactional selling, you can now put into place your own customized formula for adopting some of these same skills. Transactional selling is so important that I am currently writing an entire book on this formula. But as a value-added benefit for buying this book, here are a couple of those pages. Keep in mind that transactional selling salespeople are still on a time sensitive clock—phones are ringing and people are waiting in line.

High Conversion Transactional Selling Formula—Not a Script

1. **Answer the phone in three rings or less.** Respond to e-mails within a defined number of hours. Greet a new customer standing in line within one minute.

2. **Use an upbeat and unique greeting.** "Thank you for calling the award winning _____." My name is _____" or "Welcome to _____. I am the owner, Bill. How can I be of service?"

3. **Adjust your tone** to match the personality type of the potential buyer. At the first company I founded, we called this personality partnering. We teach four personality styles. Again for simplicity's sake, all you need to do today is to match the caller's or walk-in's tone—either super friendly (Ego/Expressive), calm and fairly monotone (Stable/Analytic), confident and direct (Dominant/Driven), or warm and caring (Amiable/Complacent).

4. **Qualify the caller or walk-in.** Find out the prospect's specific needs. You might use an approach like the following hotel example: "You said you would like a room with a king-size bed for you and your husband this Friday and Saturday, May 9th and 10th. While I am checking on that availability, may I ask what brings you to our area?"

5. **Quote four BIG benefits.** Tell the prospect why he or she should fall in love with your place of business. In this case, I will continue to use a hotel example: "You said that  you and your husband are coming for the Tomato Festival this weekend. I would like to share with you that we are only a half mile from the festival, so you can park here and avoid any parking challenges. We are a full service hotel complete with a gourmet dining room and two lounges. There are free beverages and snacks nightly in our manager's reception, and we also have an indoor pool and health club facility." Note that our hotel person quoted leisure activity benefits and not business-natured ones like free Internet service or the 24-hour business center.

6. **Offer two options and ask to confirm.** "I see that I have several options available for you. Featuring a king-size bed, we have our suite on the top floor which includes a whirlpool tub and separate living room, along with a 50-inch plasma TV. I also have another room that does

not have the separate living room, but is complete with free coffee service, nightly turndown and a 42-inch plasma TV. The suite sells for $185 per night and the king bedded room is $139. May I go ahead and confirm one of those options for you?"

7. **Be ready with a resistance question.** If the buyer does not buy, find out why. "I'm sorry. Is there something I failed to mention, or something else you might be looking for?" Make it your fault they did not buy.

8. **Offer fallback options.** Overcome objection with additional benefits that address the customer's concerns. Offer a different room option at a different price if that is what he or she needs.

There are 19 skills needed to get the most difficult buyers to buy. You just read the eight most important ones. Because understanding all 19 will require that you understand more of the science and art behind how the formula works, look for my new book on this specific topic. Before you do, implement the eight skills listed. Some of you may not need all 19 skills.

There are a few variables that determine how many and which skills get implemented. None of the 10,000 or so clients I have worked with could handle any more than five to eight skills in the beginning. That is why I have only discussed the most important eight in the formula. Additional skills can be added as individual selling models are perfected.

In the title of the previous section, I said this was not a script and some of you may be reading it as such. The formula steps are highlighted. Those steps can happen at any time during sales or service transactions depending on what the potential buyer has already expressed in terms of wants and needs, so you can adjust the formula to suit the specific needs of the customer with just TWO exceptions. Obviously, answering a call in three rings or less has to happen first. Beyond that, never ever quote a price before quoting benefits. Building value comes before the price. Why? If you quote the price first, the customer may be thinking why so high; why so little; or how does this compare to the other place I just called. If you are talking about benefits while the customer is pondering all this information, you run the risk of that person not hearing or understanding your true value proposition.

After you have the formula that works for your product or service developed, you should construct value-benefits presentations with all of your staff. What do they feel are the biggest and best reasons to buy your wares? You will need unique value-benefits presentations for different kinds of buyers. In conjunction with your entire staff, develop verbiage that works for them and works for you. Not everyone wants to say the same things the same way. They don't have to as long as it fits the formula and is acceptable to all concerned. Practice these words until your staff can't stand it any longer. This investment will pay dividends to you, your company, the buyer and the employee. Everyone wins here.

Lastly, in the hotel world, I see conversion rates of 19-40 percent, with most hotels averaging around 30 percent. That means seven out of 10 callers don't buy. They didn't buy because employees didn't follow this formula or they didn't have the right mind-set that we discussed earlier in the chapter. With 72 percent of all reservations still being made over the phone at most hotels (50 percent of people who searched the Web still call), there is a huge wasted opportunity to increase sales and market share.

The conversion rate in the hotel world should be between 70 and 80 percent. If it is higher, then the hotel's prices are likely too low. This would mean an extra $80-100,000 to a small hotel and $100-300,000 to a medium-sized hotel. I've seen a $1 million gain by some resorts and many millions at contact centers all because my clients elected to take advantage of this easy-to-capture business before a competitor figured it out. People, like

WALK INS

7 out of 10 caller

19% - 40%

30% ave.

you and me, shop around for the best value, and we are starving for someone to care enough to do it right. This formula and mind shift is what we are looking for when, as buyers, are in transactional selling situations. Consider the purchase of a car battery from an AutoZone counter. Implement this customer-centric formula and watch buyers get happier and more loyal while revenues increase. Do you think AutoZone knows its conversion rates from phone calls, e-mails, or walk-ins? Do you know yours?

Relationship Selling

Relationship selling is where one business sells to another (referred to as B-to-B). A salesperson calls on organizations that he or she feels will buy the business' product or service. They make forays into the market with the following techniques:

- Making cold calls (no appointment) by just stopping into an organization's office and asking if they have any business. Don't listen to those people who say that making cold calls is a waste of time. The right mix of cold calls is necessary for any heartily producing sales effort.

- Obtaining potential buyer lists from resources that can give highly targeted contact data for potential buyers and then sending them an e-mail (not spam) or a direct mail piece to get them to call.

- Working existing files of clients who have used the salesperson's products or services in the past by making a phone call or calling to set personal appointments.

- Having a telemarketing company prospect leads so that the calls made are pre-qualified. The salesperson then phones, e-mails or visits the business in person.

- Use advertising and marketing via any of the mediums in the marketplace such as TV, radio, newspapers, trade journals, Web sites, etc. Marketing either gets the potential buyer to call or at least warmed up to receive contact from a salesperson.

However the sales call is made, it is always the intent to make a sale as soon as you are able. But in situations where you are initiating sales contact, you more than likely are establishing a *relationship* that will advance to the point where a sale is eventually made. If your business services the account like it should be serviced and you deliver more than the customer expects then you have the *beginning* of the desired loyal client relationship.

V=D/E

This is a formula that shows how we as consumers calculate the value of something. You should memorize it and put into practice at all times. In fact, get a tattoo so you don't forget it.

V Stands for Value

This is the value as perceived by the customer not what the salesperson thinks it should be.

Before you ever called the cable company, you expected a certain level of service. If you choose a number from 1-10 for "E" or your expectation (with 10 being the best), you most likely will give the cable company a one. I hope you get better service, but this is the typical response when I question my clients. Choose a number for "D" based on what was actually delivered.

Ideally, you always deliver more than the consumer expects. So as you make your sales calls, your "D" should be greater than the "E." Always deliver more than the customer expects. The prospective buyer now becomes a buyer and uses your services. He is more impressed than he thought he would be because you delivered more than what was expected. That's the challenge—to always exceed expectations. It is just the beginning and not the end of gaining true loyalty. This same V=D/E formula applies to employer/employee relationships. Employers should deliver more than employees expect, and employees should deliver more than the employer expects. If not, divorce between the employer and employee is imminent.

So now you are ready to make your initial sales call, either via e-mail, phone, or in person, and you have your V=D/E mental mind-set going for you. You care about the employees and family members who are counting on you to bring home the bacon and you care about creating a loyal relationship with this potential client. You hopefully care more than your competition does. You know what your competition has done for the customer, what they have said, and what they have provided (see how later on in this book). You even know which competitive salespeople have called on this prospect. You know your competing salesperson's name; what they look like; what they said; and how they said it (again, you will learn how later in this book). Now you know how to present better value. You are going to be honest and customer centric. You will practice the Platinum Rule and communicate how the prospective buyer wants you to communicate. You are ready to begin your call. The ideal selling formula for building business-to-business relationship involves the following preparation:

Do your homework. Know what the prospects have bought before and how much they paid. If you don't know what they paid, you can get a pretty good idea from knowing where they've purchased in the past. I see a lot of salespeople ask prospects what kind of budget they are working with. Even those clients with larger than usual budgets almost always say they are limited. Don't ask for the amount of their budget, ask where they have purchased before. This will help you be better than your competition.

Know who (the person) the prospects bought from, and how they closed the sale. If you have been in your market for a while, you should know what your competing salespeople look like; how they say things and in what tones; and even how they dress. If you don't, I strongly suggest you invite them to lunch to see if the two of you can network leads that you refer to each other . When you go to social affairs where your competition is also in attendance, spend time with them. I've gone so far as to put up photos of competing salespeople on my office wall, so that my sales staff and I could be constantly reminded that those people are calling on our clients.

I read some time ago that in World War II there were researchers working for the German army that studied the American generals. They were trying to uncover any habits that they could use to predict an action or reaction. What they came up with was the fact that General George Patton was such a historian that he consulted battlefield history books going back hundreds of years before he ever constructed a plan of his own. These researchers were right, but thankfully, Hitler did not believe that the research could predict Patton's movements.

Know how you compare with your competition. Ask the client what things the competition offered that were exceptional. The same goes if you lose business to a competitor. You want to know why and to whom you lost it, so that you can tweak or change your approach in the future. That V=D/E formula you saw earlier came from a client who bought my training over a competitor's training, but he really liked the formula and wanted to know why we did not offer the same information. We did, starting that day, because the formula was an easy one to remember, and it conveyed a great message. It seemed like the competitive masses were copying my approach, or attempting to, wherever and whenever they could. It felt good to finally get something of value from my competition.

If you know someone, that knows your potential client, ask that person about personality type and if the prospect has any interests or hobbies that you can use in the warm-up step.

Warm up. Start your visit with something that makes a personal connection such as a common hobby or interest. Show potential clients that you are really concerned about them, not just their business. When you follow up, you can tap into this common bond as the real "personal glue" that joins this soon-to-be-loyal relationship together. If you have to fake liking someone, then get a different job.

Personality partner. I stated in the homework phase that you will try to find out the personality type of the person with whom you will be talking. What you are doing here is practicing the Platinum Rule where you use a

tone that compliments the person with whom you are communicating. When you do this, you get the prospect feeling more comfortable with you. He or she likes you, which will lead to trusting you enough to buy from you. How many times have you spoken with someone that you genuinely liked right off the get-go. The chances are pretty good that the person had a personality similar to yours and your brain said, "I really like her. She is a borderline genius. In fact, she reminds me a lot of me."

Do you want to communicate on a higher level with your clients, potential clients, employees, boss, and loved ones because you want them to do what you think needs doing? Then personality partner with them. Words are important, but how you say them is even more important because that is what people will remember.

What I recommend is that you listen for voice tones. Even if you don't remember the four classifications of personalities, remember to match tone. If a customer is upbeat and happy, you should be too. If she is direct and confident, match that style. However, be careful not to respond in a negative or pessimistic fashion even if your prospect is showing a doom and gloom attitude.

What follows is a "taste" of what personality partnering is all about, and you need more of this education if you want to be at the top of your game.

Personality Styles

Dominant/Driven personalities are direct, confident, and demanding. These people scare you. But once you find out that these are the easiest people to sell, you will welcome this style more than some others.

Dominant/Drivens are good at running companies. They like to be in charge and they are sometimes never happy with the current results—always looking to do better.

"Stand up/notch back" is the technique most effective with these folks. Be confident and look them in the eye.

Stand up to them, but don't let them feel as though they have lost control. Match their level of intensity and show a "can do" attitude.

Ego/Expressive personalities have a lot of confidence and are willing to talk to anyone and everyone. They are good salespeople and artists— fun-loving people who embrace the experience and the journey, as much if not more than, the final result.

"Stroke/take charge/ stroke" is the best technique with these folks. In other words, have fun and be real. Be the expert they want you to be and leave them as a friend. Talk to them like a brother or sister and they will welcome you. Ask questions about them.

Stable/Analytic personalities are resistant to change and they are calculating kinds of people. Accountants and engineers typically fall in this category. While the Ego/ Expressives are open, talkative, and gregarious people with all kinds of voice inflections, Stable/Analytics are more often monotone and conserve words.

"Show them/don't tell them" is the best technique for Stable/Analytics. If you are on the phone with them, use a steady voice and describe your product or service with a lot of specifics details. Paint pictures for them.

Amiable/Complacent personalities can be the toughest customers. They like to be liked, and they don't want to offend you. In your conversations with Amiable/Complacents, you may hear that everything is going well, but in their minds, they may be leaning towards not buying. It has been estimated that 55 percent of North Americans are Amiable/Complacent. I grew up in New York City and I would say that percentage is high for that region. However, small, rural towns in the Southeast might experience greater than 55 percent.

"Warm and friendly/Ben Franklin/pinch of dominance" is the best technique to be used with Amiable/Complacents. If you have to fake being warm and friendly or genuinely concerned for someone, then once again, my advice is to get a job where you don't talk to people.

So, be warm and friendly and take notes on what the prospects say are important to them. Draw a big "T" on your notes page with a plus sign on the left and a minus sign on the right. On the plus side, jot down all of the things they want that you can deliver. On the right, note those things that you cannot yet handle. When they are done giving you their needs, and you are done asking more needs and wants questions, feed back to them what you heard and expand upon how you can satisfy their needs.

When reviewing the negative side of your notes, you'll want to earnestly try and move those items that you cannot yet deliver to the positive side. How? Come up with alternatives and ask if they will meet the customers' needs because you have 15 positives and two negatives for each alternative suggestion. By the way, the first self-made millionaire in America was none other than Ben Franklin. This is how he made decisions, so you are in good company by using this technique.

When adding a pinch of dominance, be careful not to put too much pressure on the situation. But in circumstances where you have only a few items left, or an item may be discontinued, or the sale will be ending soon, make sure you add some dominance to help nudge the customers a little.

Find the facts. This is the hardest skill for many salespeople to get right. In my opinion, many executives look at high-end Ego/Expressive types and hire them automatically, figuring they were born to sell. Without the right training, these talkers don't listen as well as they should. They interrupt or start talking about all the neat things they have to sell when they don't have a complete and comprehensive picture of the potential client's needs. Therefore, it is not unusual for everyone (not just Ego/Expressive) to spend more time on this one skill than any other on this list of 12. One of the biggest rookie mistakes in sales is the failure to listen well.

Wants vs. Needs

Prospective clients will say they need something, but in reality, it may be that it is something they want—not as critical as some other things they really need. It's important to make this distinction if you do not have the item they say they need. When you offer alternatives, you will find out if they really need it or if it is more of a luxury item, something they want but is not a deal breaker. I make this point because people will say they want the absolute cheapest option, and in reality, they want value. Whenever possible, they want more than they are paying for—not the cheapest.

Short Term vs. Long Term

Find out potential clients' long-term needs, not just what they have coming up in the short term. You can tell them the truth. The more you know about total needs for the year or even years into the future, the better the value proposition you can create.

Define a "Homerun"

After you have asked your prospective clients where they have done business before, you can ask them something they may have never heard: "If my company were to 'hit one out of the park,' what would we have to do to be the best you have ever worked with? It may take them a while to answer, but don't rush it. Find out what you have to do for them to be your most loyal client.

Determine if this business is right for you. Is this business something you need or want for the short and/or long term? Is it a good fit for both the potential client and you? Questions you want to ask yourself:

- Do I offer the right product or service for the potential client?

- Can I deliver more than the clients expect for the amount of money they want to pay?

- Does the business come at the right time of the year?

- Will this client be able to pay?

- If this client is one that you would like to have, but is not willing to pay as much as you need or want, can it lead to bigger things with related organizations?

- Will this client disrupt (with noise and other negative interference) your other clients?

Connect with the big-picture benefits. After you have determined all the customers' short- and long-term needs and defined a homerun, you are ready to give them feedback by sharing how you can satisfy their needs. Remember the Ben Franklin technique mentioned in the Amiable/Complacent personality types section? I like to use this technique even with other personality types. Show them your notes and review them one by one, explaining what you heard. This shows the customer that you listen and reveals anything you may have missed. This is when you should focus on the biggest differentiators between you and your competition. If you are selling a commodity—let's say, car batteries—the greatest point of difference may only be one thing. That difference may be YOU. Knowing that you are dependable, detail conscious, personable, honest and caring—someone they want to do business with—may be the biggest deciding factor. It's called your personal value proposition.

Don't forget the additional benefits. After you have made clear the four BIGGEST reasons your product or service stands out, now you can address the minor ones.

Find out about the decision-making process. Don't be bashful about asking the customers how they make their buying decisions. Do be careful not to insult. I've been on more sales calls than I care to remember where a client's salesperson would ask something like this: "So, will you be deciding on which hotel you will be using or will someone else make that decision?" To me this sounded like, "Do you wear the pants around here or will someone with some authority be making this decision?"

Ask about the process and the timeline, and your prospects will usually volunteer how they fit into the decision and who else will come into the picture. Another important point to make here is that it's best to be able to present your own proposal instead of having a potential client present your proposal to their company. You can show passion and expertise. Plus, getting personal contact with the final decision makers will be much more impressive than a competitor who left it up to someone else to close the deal.

Try a trial close. A trial close is a good way to find out if there is anything getting in the way of a "yes" answer when you ask, "May we please earn the right to handle your business?" A trial close example might sound like the following:

"We talked about the 12 big benefits to working with my company, and we talked about the one challenge that we were not yet able to overcome, Mr. Decision Maker. Do you see us being able to work together as your provider for the short and long term?"

If the answer is anything but yes, you still have work to do. Do not pass go and do not collect $200. Go to the next step.

Overcome objections. You attempted your trial close and the prospect does not say yes. You might try something like, "Mr. Decision Maker, please tell me what it would take to earn your trust and your business." You may not be able to satisfy his needs and therefore you will not get the business, but you do find out what it takes to get the business. The customer may turn out to be the wrong one for you. That's why even the best salespeople don't close all the deals.

Use a strong close. They have said yes, you have overcome all objections, so now is the time to focus on important specifics.

Determine Payment Preference
No salesperson is awesome at everything (but we should keep trying to be) and my Achilles' heel is this: I'd go out and make the biggest sale, and when my boss would ask me how the customer was going to pay, I'd have no clue. That's when I worked for someone else. As an entrepreneur, I got a whole lot better at getting this question answered since it was money directly out of my pocket.

Communication Timeline

Ask the newest clients how he wants you to follow up and talk about deadlines that need to be kept on both sides.

Follow-up Plan

What specific things will you and he do to exceed expectations and make this new partnership a homerun?

Follow up sooner than the client expects. I always tried to get my clients things a day or two sooner than I said I would—you know, under-promise and over-deliver. I just think this makes another positive impression about your ability to be trusted. Stable/Analytics and Dominant/Drivens will also be very conscious of when and how things are delivered. Also, be personal as well as professional. Any time you can show a human side in addition to the professional side, you get a step closer to creating the most loyal of relationships.

Seek to improve. After the client uses your product or service, visit him to see what it takes to be better. One of the standard operating procedures that Marriott instilled in me when I landed my first sales job was to visit the client the day following a meeting or banquet in my hotel. It impressed the client to no end and the ideas he or she offered on how to be better were fresh and immediate. Too many times the client would say they had no advice for getting better—all was splendid. Do not take that answer. Ask him or her, "If there was just one thing I could do to be better, no matter how small, what would it be?" You would be surprised how the client can come up with a couple of things he or she would share. These clients were either Amiable/ Complacent personality types or they were forced, in a good way, to really think it through. This follow-up technique would leave such a positive impression. Can you see how  this is so much better than what your competition is doing?

Always be advancing and not just continuing. Executives, managers and bosses of salespeople take note and take heed. You get frustrated because your salesperson has been making sales calls without closing enough of them. Either that salesperson is calling on the wrong people, he or she doesn't know how to make a sales call, or it may it may just be that they are doing exactly what a salesperson should be doing. If in doubt, go out on sales calls with your sales team members. If you see them using the 14 skills mentioned in this chapter and they are calling on good potential clients, then only one question remains. Are they advancing the sale or just continuing the process?

What is the difference between advancement and continuance? In some cases, your salesperson will find out that she is dealing with a private when they really need to be dealing with a colonel. But, getting to the colonel requires going through the private. Is she moving in the right direction? It is sometimes a slow process. Is there a way to advance this lead without jeopardizing a key relationship with the private? In some cases, it is unavoidable. Often you can't get to higher-ups without upsetting a few folks on the way. My thought was always, "I don't just need more friends. I need friends who are my clients."

When setting up appointments, don't say, "I will call you next week" or I will call you next Monday." Be specific and the client will be more apt to prepare for your call. Try something more like, "How does Monday at 3 p.m. sound for you?"

The truth is that you are literally stealing intel from your competition about their clients. You're not stealing clients—just yet. It takes sales calls that follow this formula to steal the business. Then it takes executing with a V=D/E mentality and *earning* loyalty from your newest client. Gaining loyalty is not something you ever stop doing. You have to keep earning it each and every day. Does it sound daunting? It can be, but I believe it to be worthwhile. This is the kind of stuff that you will be telling your grandkids about when you find yourself sitting on the front porch some day. I don't think your stories will start with, "Let me tell you how much money we made" or "Let's talk about the profit and loss statements." I think you would rather be telling them how you and your team secured a particular client and how you continued to earn his trust, his business and eventually his friendship. The fun stuff is really why we work like we do. If making the most money is the only thing that drives you, then you would probably be doing something else for a living. You really want to do good work, do it with people you respect and love, and be compensated fairly. A bonus is the opportunity to share experiences and stories with others who can benefit from them—like right now.

Remember to use the 14 skills in this chapter whether you are in the process of stealing an account from your undeserving competitor, or if you are calling on an existing account. Your calls do not differ just because you are liberating the business from your competition.

In a nutshell, when practicing ethical theft, it is perfectly acceptable to compare what prospects are currently using your product or service. There were many times I would present a proposal to buy services from my training company and then that prospect would bring in one of my competitors right after me.

I would even suggest to my prospective client that he line us all up and have us present in front of one another. That's how sure I was that my company was the best. We did our homework; we knew what it took to create a loyal relationship; and we knew how to deliver like nobody else. We were confident, and as a result, we were the most successful by far.

Look how much time it would have saved our prospective client and look at how we would have been able to keep each other "honest" in our presentations. If I said anything that the competition felt was "stretching the truth," they could challenge me right there in front of the client. How cool would that be for me and the client, because I would be ready and the client would witness that preparation real time.

How To Make Follow-up Sales Calls

You've used the 14 skills I talked about in your initial sales call, so you know a great deal about the potential client, and you have determined that this is an account that you really want and need.

Why has this account not bought anything from you yet? Could it be one of the following reasons?

- You are waiting for the client to determine his needs for the year(s).

- The client knows his needs but is waiting for other things to fall into place before he is ready to begin discussing specifics.

- You have been talking with people who help you advance the sale and now you are waiting for the committee or other individual(s) to enter into the picture.

- You didn't make the sales call you should have made or you didn't follow up like you said you would. Do you really have the confidence of the client? If not, go fix it.

- There appears to be a hidden agenda of which you and even your contacts may not be aware.

This brings to mind a large client that I was trying to "reel in" that would bring in at least a million dollars to my training company. I did my homework, and the initial meetings went very well. The individuals I worked with were high up on the food chain, so on paper, they were the right contacts. I was planning, executing, and communicating at a high level, but I was not able to get the deal closed. After a while, I wasn't even able to get a return phone call. As it turned out, the company was trying to go from being publicly traded to individually owned, and my contacts didn't know of this transition until much later in our discussions. I never did get the business, but I was convinced I had done all that we could to secure that account. Nobody at that organization got the big customer service picture, and that company is in ruins today.

When I look back, I try to imagine the pressure that someone other than me would have been under to close that deal. I was the owner. Can you imagine someone other than me having to explain to the owner why we invested so much time and energy without knowing why the client didn't buy our training services? It would be natural for a salesperson and her bosses to begin doubting her ability. So again, my recommendation is that if you are the boss and you doubt your salesperson's ability to close a deal, go see for yourself. Go out and meet with those potential clients, and see if you can close the deal. It may just be that the client has an agenda that changed or is hidden for the time being.

If unlike my example, you know the reason why the client hasn't bought from you, and you are following up according to the timeline you established with your prospect in the initial sales call, I would recommend you make each follow-up call one that the client won't forget. Avoid the standard, "Hey Mr. Client, it's just me. I'm calling again to see if you have made a decision." Instead consider doing the following:

Make the follow-up call a service call. In other words, you check on something else that impacts the client's decision to use your services. You are actually helping the prospective buyer.

As an example, you are trying to book the National Association of Mothers of Twins Convention. You are waiting for the convention planners to determine dates based upon the availability of the keynote speaker that they really want.

You find out that the speaker they want is former first lady Laura Bush, so you do some checking. You find out which speakers bureau knows her availability and you call to get confirmation that she is available on the dates discussed. When you call your potential client, it now becomes a service call that went above and beyond the buyer's expectations.

Make your follow-up sales calls educational. You share something new with the client like a benefit you failed to mention in earlier discussions. Maybe it's a new detail that has just come to your attention, like being able to offer something even better than what was originally requested.

Be memorable. Maybe a little humor (especially if your contact is Ego/Expressive) is something that sets you apart in your message. I always had this quirky idea that I never wanted to wear a name badge in my hotel because if a guest needed to see my name tag to remember me, then I was forgettable, and that was unforgiveable.

One client requested I deliver a keynote speech at his event, so I made a few mystery shop calls to his property in order to get a better "feel" for my audience. I was pretending to be someone looking for a hotel room for the coming weekend. As he was trained to do, the front desk agent got my name and then was qualifying me by asking what was bringing me to the area. I responded that unfortunately, I was coming with my wife to visit my in-laws. He laughed and responded, "Oh Mr. Farrell, I checked my availability, and I see here that, *unfortunately*, we do have rooms." I laughed and he laughed. If I was a real customer, I would have made that reservation. I played this call for an audience of about 2,000 people during my keynote, and the front desk agent received a resounding applause for tuning into me and turning me on by being memorable.

Chapter II: You Can't Steal Loyal Clients or Loyal Employees

In previous chapters I talked about how to have the right mind set to make sales calls; the difference between transactional selling and relationship selling; and even how to make follow-up sales calls, but I need to be clear about something. If you or your competitors have done

what is supposed to be done, then clients and employees will not leave because they will remain loyal. The good news/bad news is that very few organizations pull this off. Companies can talk a good game with their mission, vision and value statements, but they just don't deliver as advertised. If they did, you would be getting better service today in America and in the rest of the world, instead of the poor service reality we generally face as consumers.

This brings to mind another story. It is the late '80s and before my training company was born. I was doing consulting work for a pretty large number of clients, because I *guaranteed* them that my work would produce a certain amount of money in a very specific time frame or they would not have to pay me—not one dime. I was the only one I knew that was willing to guarantee anything in the consulting world.

I was in a secondary market in Ohio making sales calls on accounts that my client's hotel used to have but lost. With my client's sales manager, I was calling on a company that makes rubber hoses and conveyor belts. This call was so memorable to me that, to this day, when I walk on a rubber speed walk at airports or pump gas, I check the markings. Almost inevitably, it is made by this company. It was the largest account my client's hotel ever had and they had it for many years. They lost the account six months prior to my arrival. The rubber company contact was good enough to take my call and set up an appointment to see us face-to-face later that week. Here is what he said when we got there:

- We used your hotel for more than 10 years, and we think we were a pretty big account, but you treated us as though you did not need us or want us.

- Our employees and our customers would stay at your hotel and come to the front desk for directions to our building. Your front desk staff did not know, nor did they attempt to find out.

- We know what the hotel business is about, yet your hotel's employees have no idea what our company does, nor do they even care to find out.

This gentleman looked me in the eye and asked me, "Does this sound like a place where you would want to do business?" I told him no and asked him to share with us what hotel he was currently using and some of the things they were doing to earn his business.

After sharing a very long list of things that my competing hotel was offering, I told him that we would not call on him again until we felt like we had earned the right to do so.

Immediately after this meeting, I asked the sales manager to take me to this competitive hotel where I walked and talked with the employees. Believe me. They knew a lot about this rubber company. It was a better physical hotel, and now they had the service turned up high. They were well on their way to loyalty.

I need to state this plainly and succinctly. The only chance you have of stealing business or employees away from your competition if they have true loyalty is if they lose that loyalty. How would they lose it? Here are a few ways:

- The people in charge or those who drive a loyalty culture move on to a different job or a different location, and then the folks that follow them do not practice what they've learned. You can now swoop in and be the new loyal provider. Later in this book, you will hear how to get your competition's loyal culture drivers hired away faster.

- The client has a dramatic change of events within his own organization. He finds himself not being able to spend the kind of money he used to spend with the current provider. If you can provide, at the dramatically lower price point, and still deliver loyalty, you have a chance at liberating this business.

- A competitor that does a great job of providing loyalty may only exert this effort to his top accounts. That leaves all of his other accounts at risk.

So my take away from this chapter is that you need to focus your liberating efforts on those competitors who you know do not offer the loyalty-building kind of customer service for all of their accounts. Keep tabs on these loyalty-producing competitors, so when the day comes that they slip, you are there to liberate.

The other take away point is that competitors may have this same focus. Assume others are looking at your business the way that you salivate over their business—no room for slip-ups and errors. Love your accounts, love your employees, and always be working toward creating a loyalty-building culture.

Losing Good Employees Is Like Losing a Good Account

If you lose a good employee, than you deserve to lose a good employee *unless* they leave because of personal or professional advancement that you could not match.

If I lost a great employee for an opportunity I thought was better than what I could provide, than I would tell the employee just that. I would then try to hire them back in a year or two when they have learned new skills working for someone else—skills they may not have learned working for me. I would also tell them, in advance, that my plan is to hire them back someday. This is quite the incentive for that employee to learn more and keep in touch.

Other employees and clients identify with people more

than the product, so when you lose a good person, you lose a little of your product's soul. So if you have to lose an employee, make sure your clients and those employees left behind know why you lost them. Share with them the steps you are taking to make sure you don't let anything slip. Remind them that you are still and always committed to keeping their loyalty.

You have to ask yourself, would you rather lose a manager who is very good, but not necessarily connected to your clientele, or would you rather lose a salesperson who is very well thought of by your clients? I would say the manager. So managers, hear this loud and clear—get customer centric and get closer to the people who are part of your accounts. If you are harder to replace, you are worth more, and your operation will run better when you are on the front lines with your accounts. Being on the front line means you hear and see more, and will do more as a result.

I was a keynote speaker for an association of hospitality hospital homes. This is a neat collection of about 100 homes and buildings spread throughout the United States that house and take care of patients' families for little or no expense to the families.

I finished my keynote and was going to be conducting a workshop later that day, so I sat in on some other presentations. The one workshop I attended was telling its listeners how to recruit volunteers and then hang onto them longer. As the speaker was getting into her talk, it occurred to me that she was using similar ideas that I throw out to audiences on how to hang onto great employees longer. The difference was that I liked her mind shift a little bit better than mine. How much happier, how much better, and how much more successful would businesses be if we treated our employees like they were volunteers? Another way to assess your business' culture is to ask yourself, "How would I treat my employees differently if they were my best account?"

Those Who Steal For You Will Steal Against You

I can't tell you where I first heard this little proverb because it was so long ago. I also can't remember too many of my salespeople leaving me while I worked directly in the hotel business. On the contrary, I surely saw what happened when employees left my training business. I made sure that any terrific salesperson that worked for me was taken care of in many ways, so that I would not lose them and have to compete against them in my market.

In my training company, we had 265 employees and licensees in 44 countries. In the more than 20 years that I was an owner, we probably trained well over 10,000 new clients. We were then, and they still are today, the largest and best sales and service training company in the world (www.signatureworldwide.com).

Being a trainer is difficult, especially when married or a parent, because trainers often left their homes on a Sunday night to return late Thursday or even Friday. Doing

this week in and week out is tough on a family, and I had estimated we would hang onto trainers for only two years before they would not want to sacrifice time away from their family any more. As it was, we held onto them a lot longer than that. For many, they loved the job but could not do the traveling. As a result, some went to work for our clients as trainers, or they started up their own training company where the return on their investment would justify the time away from home.

A double whammy—you lose a client and a trainer. How do you tell your client not to steal your trainers? My team had more than a few discussions about how to prevent this from happening including making it illegal, but that negative spin just did not seem to be the best way to go. Instead, we opted to make the clients understand (in most cases they saw the light). By hiring our company, they got so much more than just a trainer, and that was true. But, it didn't always work. Today, the team at Signature runs into ex-trainers who are now competitors selling to the same

clients. Those who will steal for you will steal against you, so here is how to combat that problem:

- Try not to lose your employees.

- Try to get your clients to see that they are buying a whole company, not just a salesperson. The best way to do this is to have the "top dogs" at your company visit with and establish a relationship with your clients. Newsletters and marketing pieces are good, but nothing beats making a face-to-face connection.

- Always be looking for great employees that want to be liberated from their current jobs, especially those working for your competition. They can bring business, new ideas, and fresh perspectives.

I read recently about one major car company suing another over intelligence that its ex-employees took to the competition. I am certainly not an attorney, so I don't know how this will turn out with the courts. From a layman's point of view, unless these ex-employees delivered copyrighted, protected practices, or patented items that the other company used, I can't see where there was harm nor foul. ■

Chapter III: Tactical Stealing Stories

Want Ads

Advertise for a salesperson or manager in your market and feeder markets (those close geographical places from which you get business), even if you don't need them at

the moment. Anyone who works for the competition who contacts you looking for a job, interview him or her. Interview a lot.

I've had more people than I care to mention actually bring me their company's marketing and business plans. I would review these plans, talk in detail with the person who brought them, and then give the plans back to that person and send him on his way. I wouldn't hire this person in a million years for several reasons:

- I want them working for my competition.

- Those who will steal for you will steal against you, and I couldn't trust this person.

- There are more professional ways of presenting yourself, and I only hired professionals or professionals-in-the-making.

Those folks you've interviewed in the past, that you liked a lot, now give you instant access to replacements for folks you will lose in the future.

Even though you were not looking to replace a salesperson or manager, you may run across someone who adds so much return on investment to your organization that you will create a new position for that person. In essence, you are investing in new resources.

If you are the person being interviewed and you work for the interviewer's competition, be professional. Do not give away too much. Make it clear that you know your stuff, but hold back on details. You still owe your current employer a certain amount of respect, even though you probably feel she doesn't deserve you.

Keep in mind that the person sitting across from you is visualizing you doing this same thing someday with her competition, so you need to explain, very specifically, why and how this will not happen. Give the reasons you want to leave your current employer. Reassure the interviewer that you will be content in a position with her company as long as those same things don't happen.

Call Accounting

OK, this is where you start to come to grips with how far you are willing to go with this ethical stealing concept. If you are not willing to do this—and I understand why—at least  keep it from happening to you. I get queasy when I tell people this story, so you can imagine how I feel when I am leaving it to the interpretation of many who will read it. But, here goes.

The stage needs to be set because I believe the dynamics need to be understood and appreciated. Most organizations that have a sales department also have an accounting department. Ego/Expressives verses the Stable/Analytics. Many are the days when these groups do not see the world the same. They both seem to keep the other in check—to the point where, in most of the hotels at which I have worked, there was an unhealthy dislike or distrust of one another.

Remember me telling you earlier in this book that I was not very good at finding out how my clients were going to pay their bills? To an accountant, this is like not wearing your shoes and socks. How could I not make this the first question for which I would get an answer? I can certainly see why I was not on the accounting Christmas card list.

On the other hand, if we ever sent our accounting folks out into the world and told them not to come back until they found business, there would be a lot of wing-tipped-shoed, wool-suit-in-July-wearing, Volvo- driving introverts who would not be coming back any time soon.

However, there is this underlying understanding between the two groups that the other is at best, a necessary evil. Given that knowledge, here is one of the very first things that I would do (with great success) as soon as I arrived at a new hotel or began working as a consultant with a new client. I would call the accounting department. You only get one shot per location to do this right, so lock yourself in a room and be ready to go. Here's how it would work.

I would call up the switchboard at my competing hotel and ask whoever answered the phone for the name of the person who handles accounts receivable. I would then ask to be transferred to that person. I would keep calling back until I got that person. I would not leave a message, and I would make sure that my number would not register on caller ID (not usually an issue with most accounting offices, especially since the call is transferred).

Mr. Accounting would answer in his best Stable/Analytic "I have more important work to do than talking to live human beings" tone. In fact, it was usually an "I got into this business so I would not have to talk to you" voice.

In my best Stable/Analytic monotone voice, I would introduce myself as the chief financial officer (CFO) of a major corporation—one that I knew was not in their market. I would know that this is the real CFO's name in the event Mr. Accounting actually read some financial news and knew the name of the company's CFO. That never happened, but I did not want any screw-ups.

I tell Mr. Accounting that the reason I am calling is because we are about to announce plans to build a major training center in his area. We will be in need of hotel accommodations for everyone from our construction crews, to employees, to our clients for years to come. We think it will mean hundreds of thousands of dollars, if not a million dollars, in the first year alone. I was careful not to use too much hotel jargon.

I go on to tell Mr. Accounting that I would rather talk to him than a salesperson because—drum roll please—I don't trust salespeople, and that I would much rather work with someone like me.

I would always get this vision of his mouth agape, followed up by a lot of fist bumping, body twisting and turning (also known as dancing) in his office. He has never ever, even remotely, received a phone call like this one before, and it is refreshing for him to hear that the "outside" world shares his view of those vermin salespeople.

He would fumble with the next few sentences, but in essence get around to asking me what it is I needed from him.

I would go on to say, "Mr. Accounting, what I need from you is a list of references that I will personally call. I need company names, contact names, phone numbers and an idea of how big they are for you, so I am only calling like-sized accounts."

You may not believe me, but I have been on the phone with accounting folks who get to the tenth reference. I tell them that I have plenty, and yet they won't let me hang up. They insist on giving me more. They also interject their payment histories too.

After I do hang up, I have this mental vision of Mr. Accounting jetting out of his assigned space and risking life and limb in the search for the general manager to offer up the great news. One additional note here: I can count on two fingers how many times the accounting person asked how they could reach me in order to follow up.

So to all of the accounting people who kicked my $800 expense reports back to me because I did not attach a $1.29 McDonald's receipt, this is my payback.

To those managers and salespeople who are running down to their accounting offices right about now, be nice. You need accounting people to find out how your clients will be paying.

Buy the Relationship

If there is an organization that you know has enough business to warrant buying its product or service, then it's a real win/win for both of you.

I was working as a director of sales at my first hotel in suburban Chicago and like many of your "firsts," this hotel was not ideal. Physically, it could not compare favorably to my four other primary competitors.

I get a lead for a huge piece of training business, and I know that my competition probably got the same lead at about the same time. The potential client is value conscious and has an image-conscious brand. My hotel brand is a notch below what you would assume would be on its short list of hotels.

The day arrives when the potential client would like to tour my hotel and those of my competitors. Following the selling skills outlined in chapter four, I sat with the decision maker to document all of her needs, and there was more than my hotel could handle.

I knew we were talking about a considerable amount of business that would make this account the largest in our hotel. I told her that we could tour and she would see that we could not handle her needs, or we could sit and talk about all the stuff I would buy from her company to convert sleeping rooms into customized-to-her-needs meeting rooms. With all of these new meeting rooms,  we would be the best of all options when compared to the competition.

We spent $250,000 with her company to acquire an account that brought in $2.5 million in the following two years. Best yet, was that we were able to use those meeting rooms for other clients and make additional revenues for many years to come.

I helped her imagine how she would be a hero when she went back to her bosses with an order for $250,000 worth of business to offset the $2.5 million they would have spent at any hotel.

It does not have to be as big or as dramatic of an investment. Switching to a provider that offers you business without sacrificing quality or price is a slam dunk way to buy new friends.

Salute to Industry

You take a public area of your building and dedicate that space to thanking existing business. This provides an opportunity to demonstrate your willingness to help potential clients. Here is a personal example of how this has worked.

I was working at a large hotel in St. Louis, and I noticed that we had a lot of space that got a lot of public foot traffic which went unnoticed. We calculated how many people attended meetings or walked by these areas on their way to their sleeping rooms. We even counted how many people just walked by this area on their way to the bathrooms.

With those pretty hefty-sized numbers (that surprised us too), we now figured out why the carpet wore out so fast. We took those numbers, and with pictures of the area, went to our top six accounts.

We always thanked our accounts for their business. We tried to remember their birthdays, their kids' names, and other stuff to show our appreciation.

We now had a new way to show how much we cared for them. We wanted to provide thousands of square feet in our hotel to display their product or service. We wanted to rope that area off and post an attractive sign explaining what they do and how to contact the company in the event that one of our customers would like to be their customer too.

We explained that we think this is an ultimate way to thank them for their business by providing them with more business opportunities. After 30 days of displaying their product or service, we wanted to have a cocktail reception around the display during which we would take a photo to be framed and hung on a wall for all to see for years to come.

We did this for six months for our top six accounts, and for the other six months, we asked *big* potential accounts that we had already been courting to be on our "Salute to Industry" wall of fame too. We told these prospects that this is one of the many things we do to show appreciation, and that if they stayed with us, they would have to get used to this kind of treatment.

I thought we would have to construct these displays ourselves, but what happened was amazing. We had companies set up their tradeshows displays or send construction crews to build beautiful displays. Anheuser-Busch sent in a design team, then a decorator and then the construction crew. These clients were thinking bigger than I was, and I loved it.

Another cool benefit was that I had companies, who I never heard of, accidently run into one of these displays and want to pay me to display their goods and services. We never took it that far, but it was nice to know that we could have.

Get 'em Gone Using Headhunters

It's time to take another deep breath and see how far we push your ethics meter. Headhunter is a term we use to describe those folks who specialize in recruiting expert talent for their clients. They typically work on commission to find senior management and highly specialized positions including salespeople. These headhunters are usually contact heavy—knowing a lot of people with which they can network. The best ones focus on market segments that they know well.

It makes for a good day the first time you get a call from a headhunter saying that "someone" recommended you for a position and they would like to talk to you more about it.

You think about the last time your boss said that you did such a good job that you should be promoted. This call from your local, friendly super recruiter is something for which you will find a clean page on your note pad.

After you have fielded a few of these calls, and even used one to find a new position, you begin to get to know who the specialists are and how you can use them for your gains.

Let's say you are very happy where you are working and this headhunter calls you with a specific job in mind. This is your chance to get a high-performing, competing salesperson hired away from your primary competition. You tell your headhunter that you are not interested, but that he should call so and so over at your competition. This especially makes sense if it gets your competing salesperson hired into an entirely different market.

The more leads I gave headhunters, the more they called me. I have a favorite hotel headhunter who used to be my boss when I was too young to take clients into my own bar. If you e-mail me, I will give you his contact information. Did you like that Peter?

A few headhunters would even let me know ahead of time that they placed a new salesperson with one of my competitors and would share that person's resume with me so I knew who was about to come into the neighborhood. We would welcome that new competing salesperson even before he arrived and begin networking right away to find out if he was going to be an ally or foe and to what extent. I often wondered if the new salesperson got a better reception from us than he did from his own hotel.

I have even given the names of bosses I did not like to the headhunters that I was not particularly fond of. I can't remember if one of those attempts ever worked, but it sure made for a fun few minutes.

There were a few times I made a bad sales hire and would call up my headhunters to get them placed elsewhere. They were good salespeople but were not right for my product. So, if you get a lot of headhunting calls all of a sudden, your boss may be trying to tell you something.

Cruising for Business at the Rental Car Counters

Think about the folks who have enough credibility and may be asked to make a recommendation regarding your business—a third party person who has little to nothing to gain by referring you as a source. In the world of hotels, rental car counters are such a resource.

I was standing at a rental car counter many years ago, and I heard the gentleman ahead of me ask the agent what hotel she would recommend for the downtown area. The agent immediately went into a presentation that you could tell she had used before. She told him which hotels he shouldn't use and then recommended two options. She also provided directions on how to get to those hotels. She was very good at being an expert hotelier. In fact, better at that than she was her real job.

After I get my rental car stuff, I asked her how often that kind of an exchange occurred during a typical day and her response was astounding. I was shocked that in today's world, where you can easily get this kind of information, people still waited until the last minute.

So our salute to the rental car industry was born, and we took this show on the road (pun intended).

What we did was to print up adhesive note pads that had a drawing of our hotel on them and list of our *big* benefits. On the back was a simple map for getting to the hotel from the airport and a blank line where the rental car agent printed his or her name.

When someone asked for a hotel recommendation, the agent would whip out one of our pads and tear off a sheet explaining how cool my hotel was. The agent told the potential guests that if they presented that sheet to the front desk at our hotel, it would get them a 10 percent discount.

The guest would walk in and present the coupon. We would honor that rate provided we had a room available. That coupon would go into a filing system that kept track of who made the recommendation.

At the end of every month, I would go out to the airport during a time period that I knew would be slower, so that I could get *all* of the rental agents' attention.

I would count out brand new dollar bills—five for each person the agent sent to our hotel. It sounded something like this: "So let's see. Suzie from Avis gets 20, 21, 22, 23, … $35 this month. Thank you Suzie."

All the agents from the other rental car companies would be asking, "What's he doing? How do I make that money too?"

This would become a monthly show, and I became one of the most recognizable and popular guys at the airport— once again having to buy my friends.

If business was down at our hotel, we would make more frequent trips to the airport. We would remind the agents of our incentive and ask what we could do to get them even more excited about recommending our property. This is an example of stealing business before the competition even knows it is there.

Executive Travel Club

Loyalty club programs today are big business—offering airlines miles; hotel points good for airline miles; free stays; and gifts. The consumers who use these programs tend to do a higher volume of business. They are willing to pay more of their organization's money to get these personal benefits. I think there is a general mentality that they deserve these perks for dealing with the stress and strain of travelling. I am writing a book called "All I

Want To Do Is Fix One Airline," so I have empathy and sympathy for these road warriors.

I was once delivering a keynote address where I asked 1,000 audience members to take out their wallets and count the number of loyalty programs to which they belonged. The average was eight. Some had programs they used with competing brands. So where is the loyalty there?

Let me state for the record that frequency and "loyalty"

 programs that offer benefits for regular customers should never be a company's only attempt to provide exceptional service. If you try to mask a lack of customer service with these kinds of programs, you may get more business from your clientele, but you certainly won't be gaining loyalty. Your program will be just one of several to which the customer belongs. In other words, you won't have the kind of loyalty you need. Get your house in order and get your service levels to exceed expectations.

If you have the right value proposition and you feel your service deliverables are at the right level, then you may want to consider an executive travel club program like the one I will describe. This program will give you another level of defense against competitors who may have more recognizable brands or who offer healthy frequency programs. It will be another tool that you can use to justify charging higher rates while offering something "exclusive" to your better customers and clients.

Once you implement an executive travel club program, it is nearly impossible to take it away without causing damage to your image and credibility, so think and execute flawlessly.

For those folks that make their own buying decisions, without using an administrative assistant or travel agent, this program gives them personal and professional benefits above and beyond what the "normal" customer gets.

This was a tool I designed for our front desk agents to use when they would qualify guests and find out if they had the potential of using our hotel more often. If my hotel offered a "branded" frequency program, we would offer it and our executive travel club program. This way, our guest would be able to take advantage of two programs at the same time. This type of program only makes sense if you have a lot of similar branded products in your market fighting for the same customer.

In the spirit of getting everyone involved in the art of selling at my hotels, I liked giving the front desk agents— who might be nervous about "selling"—a tool they could use to build their confidence. They qualified who received membership into our executive travel club program and would offer incentives at different times of the year to plug more business into slower revenue periods.

The marketing piece would be kept at the front desk, and it was a smart-looking, six-panel brochure that was die cut to look like a suit and a tie. It was a marketing piece of which we were proud, and it listed all of our hotel locations so we would be promoting usage to our sister properties.

Some of the benefits called out in this brochure included:

- Guaranteed availability. We were never full for this guest.

- A guaranteed no-walk policy. If for some reason, we messed up and could not accommodate a guest's stay, we would pay for his or her room at a nearby hotel; offer transportation to that hotel; and give the guest $100 in cash for his or her troubles. This ensured that none of the executive travel club members ever walked and the hotel avoided making a premium guest unhappy.

- Cash back. After staying 10 nights, we would hand the guest cash back on his or her eleventh stay. We didn't offer a free room because this would force the guest into cheating on his or her expense report in order to get a personal benefit. We would literally hand new money back to the guest.

- Quick access to the front desk manager. We would give the guest a direct-line phone number and e-mail address for the front desk manager of each hotel. This ensured faster and better care for our best customers.

- Room upgrades when available.

This was not a discount program. These guests paid top dollar. If a guest could not pay top dollar, they could get a rate commensurate with their volume of business, but that guest was not eligible to be part of executive travel club program. This program also helped generate a great mailing list for specials when we needed business the most.

Typically, you would have a guest that might try two to three different types of hotels in your market. If this guest could not get into one because it was full, he or she had a back-up. These guests are loyal, but to two or three providers. With the executive travel club program, this shared loyalty is eliminated. Now you have a top-shelf customer needing only one solution—your hotel.

You are stealing what is rightfully yours and you are using non-traditional salespeople to help you do it. We will talk about what this does for your culture later in this chapter.

The Lodging Connection (TLC)

While the executive travel club program targeted those individuals who make their own buying decisions, the TLC program focused on those administrative assistants or travel agents who made buying decisions for their bosses or co-workers.

As my sales staff would be out making calls, they would ask who was responsible for making individual reservations. I will use the collective word administrators here for simplicity sake, but it could be one or more administrative assistants or even a travel department for larger organizations. If the administrator with whom we were talking were loyal to a competitor, we would offer her the TLC program to get her to try our hotel, and she always chose us after the offer.

We made sure we gave her the words she would want to use to communicate with her boss as to why she changed hotels. It was not because she received personal benefits.

With government accounts or companies that had a policy against employees accepting gifts from providers, we would offer to do one of the following:

- Keep a credit balance in the company's name, and at the end of the year, it could use that credit for a reception or similar function in the hotel. This would also ensure that we hosted the company's Christmas and holiday parties.

- Make a donation to the company's charity of choice each time it made a reservation.

In the interest of full disclosure, many of these administrators would tell us they were not allowed to accept gifts. They would then call us back later that day and ask us to mail the gifts to their home addresses, so we did. Someone should add up all the wasted man hours spent when companies develop these policies only to have employees work so hard to "beat the system." Companies should come to their senses and eliminate 90 percent of their policies. After all, employees eliminate them anyway.

As part of the TLC program, we would offer the administrators cash back after so many stays. They too had their own direct phone line and e-mail address to the front office manager, guaranteed availability, and 50 percent off the price of any room for their personal stay. We wanted them to experience our hotel, so we made it easy for them to bring their families for a weekend. How cool would that administrator feel sitting around the pool with her kids who would be in awe that their mom had that kind of power and got them that kind of service.

We would have quarterly TLC receptions at the hotel and invited hundreds of people. A good 70 percent would show up to these lavishly themed events. This is where we would thank them for trusting us with their bosses, their clients, and their company officials.

One particular themed event will always stand out in my mind. We had a "live" food demonstration. The food and beverage department cut holes in the middle of the banquet tables and had the wait staff stick their heads up through the holes from underneath complete with full make up (to look like the food item) so you did not know these were live human beings on platters surrounded by food. The event was set up in a buffet style, complete with the skirting, tablecloths, platters, props, garnishes and make-up. We opened the doors late to create some sense of urgency and when we would open the doors the administrators rushed in to partake. At different points in the long buffet, the wait staff would begin talking to the administrators who were piling food on their plates. Some almost had heart attacks. They were laughing and carrying on because they were afraid to touch anything for fear it would be alive. They talked about that party for over a year. We called it our "live food reception". We had competitors who copied our program and tried to copy these events, so being unique and unforgettable was part of the strategy.

Quote One Rate

I don't know if other industries outside of airlines, hotels, vacation rentals and car rentals base their rates upon availability (inventory), but if you do, please pay attention to the following story.

I had a hotel competitor located across the street that had a much better brand image for the corporate market. Physically, we could compete, but they had the better brand for driving higher rates. The problem had by our competitor stemmed from the fact that the hotel would quote a different rate for each night of a guest's stay.

Imagine if you were a meeting planner and you needed 25 sleeping rooms with a rooming list; a meeting room for 45, complete with lunches and kick-off dinner; coffee breaks in the morning and afternoon; audio visual needs; specific billing arrangements; special needs for certain individuals such as vegetarian meals and wheelchair accessible rooms; transportation needs from the hotel to your company's facilities on one day, etc. Would you really want to have to take notes on the different room rates offered for each night of the four-night stay?

This scenario does not compute for most consumers. The competitor's hotel salesperson said (smugly) that his rates are based upon availability and the busier the hotel, the greater the room rate.

Not knowing any better, this meeting planner came over to my hotel and went through the litany of needs. He told me he had been to the swanky hotel across the street, because I asked him who else he was considering.

Almost every hotel in America sets their rates based upon availability, but only the "out of touch" ones change the rate each night of a guest's stay. Thankfully for me, the leaders of the swanky hotel were not very bright. I made sure no headhunter knew who was working at the swanky hotel. In fact, I almost put that director of sales on my payroll because he was such a good salesperson for me.

I told that meeting planner there would only be one room rate that he would have to consider. He was relieved to have details minimized and made simpler for him—a refreshing customer experience.

What room rate would I quote? Let's say Hotel Swank was charging $100, $110, $120 and then $85 respectively for each night of the four- night stay. That would be a total of $415 in room charges for each guest. I would charge $110 per night for all four nights, which almost sounds better when compared to the $120 price that the director of sales quoted for his peak night. I would make $440 in room charges because the meeting planner would rather have his job made easier instead of his bill made cheaper. There is value in making things easier and simpler. ■

Chapter IV: Everyone Sells

I mentioned in the executive travel club section that I got the front desk agents involved in selling. This section is dedicated to getting everyone, and I mean everyone, to sell.

You can never ever have enough people selling your products and services—employees, customers, purveyors, friends, families, etc. How do you get them to sell for you?

Starting with your own employees, have a general assembly. As their leader, tell them that selling is their first job. Here is the message you want to deliver: NOTHING HAPPENS UNTIL SOMEBODY SELLS SOMETHING. Sometimes just asking for employees to sell is all it takes. You'll hear about employees who have neighbors working for organizations with which you would like to do business. As it turns out, your employee is living next door to the decision maker.

You should also ask your employees to contribute new ideas on how to improve revenues, how to reach new market segments, and how to offer new products. Pay a commission for business they help you book. In the hotel world, we would have gladly paid a complete stranger (like a travel agent) a 10 percent commission for every room night she would send to us. That being the case, why would I not offer my own employee at least five percent? If not a cash commission, offer another bonus item or perk that will get them excited. In most cases, the recognition and thanks alone is enough. The commission or perk is just an added nicety.

When business is down, call all the troops together again and be honest with them. Explain that you can't give them the tools they need unless you have the revenue fuel to drive the engine, so ask the employees to help you help them.

Maybe this will confirm I am an ego maniac, but I will never forget how badly I wanted to win employee of the month when I was working in the kitchen for Marriott. The problem for me was that all department heads voted monthly on who should win, and because I was limited to the kitchen, the other managers had no clue as to who I was. I found out some time later that my food and beverage director nominated me six straight months for this award, and each time he and I lost. I didn't win until I began working in the front of the house (the public areas) as a bellman.

Truth is, I probably worked harder and deserved it more as a pot scrubber. The feeling of winning and having my picture mounted in the lobby for all to see was what I was after—not the $25. This is the feeling you want to create for all employees, who in addition to doing outstanding work in their own areas, help your company grow revenues. Provide the recognition that is deserved and warranted.

Getting everyone involved in selling will create a lot more empathy. Employees will better understand how hard it is to sell and how much harder they all need to work to retain those hard-fought-for customers.

I can't think of a single business that isn't at risk of having customers and employees stolen when it does not have a sales and service culture. Even research labs, nuclear waste sites, public schools and government agencies need a customer service and sales focus.

Purveyor Calls

Purveyors are the folks from whom you already buy. If asked, they can and should do more. Purveyors typically think they already owe you because you provide them with revenues, but I don't think the best way to get more out of them is to rub their nose in it.

I would see our bakery delivery guy (one example of many) bringing in all kinds of breads and cakes. As a salesperson, I would go up to him when he got a break and ask if he wanted a cup of coffee or anything else. He would be stunned that I offered.

Over a cup of coffee, standing in the corner of the kitchen, I would ask him about the other companies to which he delivered goods. I would ask him how busy these places were. I would mention how terrific these places were as competitors and explain how we loved the competition. Eventually, at some point in the conversation, he would share with me that so and so is developing a new menu, or he would tell me about some new refurbishing another competitor was about to undertake. These purveyors know stuff.

After a couple cups of coffee, over the span of a few months, I would get bolder. I would ask these purveyors to keep an eye out for leads, because the busier we were, the more bakery products we would buy. If a cup of coffee wasn't enough to persuade the purveyor, I would buy him a prime rib dinner or buy dinner for his whole family. Once again, here is a dad with his kids who were eating for free in a terrific restaurant that also served his baked goods. Everybody is impressed.

Teach all of your managers how to have this kind of conversation. It's not just for the salespeople.

Sales Blitzes

This is absolutely a must for any and all businesses. A sales blitz is a concentrated selling effort in which many of your employees try to find new business.

Itissuchapowerfultoolandreturnoninvestmentdriverthat I have mapped out the development of a new company which helps clients conduct and then properly follow up on sales blitzes. That's how much of an impact these initiatives can be.

Let's do the math. You have three people selling in your sales office. They each say they make 30-50 qualified calls a week (over the phone and in person) on average. But upon further review of their math, you see that they make closer to 20 qualified calls per week. Twenty calls a week multiplied by three salespeople equals 60 calls a week total. Multiply that by 50 weeks a year. That's a grand total of 3,000 calls per year. We won't even get into how many were new accounts or new contacts, or how many will generate business.

Make a list of your three salespeople. Add in your five other department managers (especially the organization's leader) and eight other personable employees. That is 16 employees or eight teams of two.

If eight teams made 25 sales calls each for a four-day period, that would equate to 800 sales calls in less than one week versus the 60 calls that the sales office was currently making. Eight hundred calls represents more than a quarter of the sales calls your operation normally makes in a year. Complete four sales blitzes a year and you double the production of your sales department.

Pair up all 16 people—eight people who have made sales calls before with the other eight employees who are willing to potentially buddy up with one of the managers. Partnering will create additional incentive to make as many calls as possible.

Now that you see the wisdom in the effort, here is how to conduct a sales blitz that will produce a considerable return on investment:

- First know that most sales blitzes fail due to ineffective follow-up, so plan for the follow-up and not just the blitzing sales calls.

- If this is your first sales blitz, determine if you should work geographically or by market segment. For hotels, retail establishment, and other service-based businesses, you'll find that calling on clients closest to your location is best.

- Your primary mission for the blitz is to uncover leads that you didn't know existed. You'll need to follow up on these leads to set appointments for a proper sales call. Secondly, you'll want to spread the word in your market that you have benefits in which others may be interested—keeping your business top-of-mind.

- The call itself is very simple and would sound something like, "I realize I'm calling without an appointment, but I simply want to know if you have a need for our services. If so, who may I call in the future in order to discuss our unique benefits?" Many times, the gatekeeper, receptionist, or counter person will tell you with whom you need to speak and that person may even agree to see you for a few minutes.

- Sometimes, in the hotel industry, we would have a reception around our pool at the end of that week and invite those people with whom we spoke and their guests. We would take groups on tours of the back and front of the house. They always loved seeing what the public does not get to see—the kitchens and the  housekeeping and maintenance areas. Meanwhile, the competition wouldn't do this because their insurance agent convinced them that someone would sue if they slipped and fell. I took that chance a hundred times or more and nobody ever sued my hotels.

- We would blitz as the busy season would near an end, and this blitz would find us business for the slower season. We would blitz if we were doing major renovations, and we would blitz when we felt like the competition was getting too close to copying us.

- Some of the sales calls reach people who want to work for you. You may even spot a terrific employee that you want to liberate at some point in the future.

- The managers and employees, who normally don't make outside sales calls, have a refreshed and renewed respect for how challenging it is for the sales team, and more empathy usually equals better service.

- You can either set up your blitz for cold calls or send out a marketing piece ahead of time telling your prospects that you are coming and will make it worth their time and courtesy. The marketing piece warms them up.

- Have daily recap meetings to keep everyone accountable and energized. Making 25 sales calls a day for four straight days is mentally and physically draining, especially for those that don't sell as their primary job function. Have fun with these meetings— laugh about the experiences, give kudos, eat pizza, and drink beer with the team. On the last day, hand out awards for most calls, best call, funniest call, etc. You can also treat the group to a fine dinner. You want them to want to be included in the next blitz.

- Reduce all leads to a database that can be used for timely follow up. Calculate return on investment. Don't be surprised if you get a rush of new business immediately following the first day of calls. I can't tell you how many times I would get inundated with new business, and when I asked those new customers if they had seen some of our folks that week during a sales blitz, they would have no idea what I was  talking about. It is almost cosmic how business finds you when you put forth the effort in a big way. I realize that "cosmic" statement probably raised an eyebrow, but do a blitz and you will see what I mean.

- If you don't have enough employees to conduct a blitz of this size, then conduct a smaller blitz or ask your local university for help. If you approach the marketing department, entrepreneurial department, or some department related to your field for personable students to help you make sales calls, you should find lots of support. It is great experience for the student. Plus, now you have these students running around talking about your cool company and you find potential employees.

I loved taking a nervous employee with me on calls. Let's call her nervous Norma. She would tell me in the car, or as we were walking to our first call, that she was really nervous and that she expected me to do the talking. I would assure her that I would and that she had nothing

to worry about. Her job was to sit there and look good. Norma is relieved. After introducing ourselves to someone who could use our services, I would say this, "Mr. Potential Buyer of My Services, my name is Don and my associates' name is Norma. You two are the important ones here. I may book your business, but Norma is the key because she will take care of you. So, Norma, please tell Mr. Potential Buyer what you do at the hotel."

Norma might stutter and stammer, but what came out of her mouth was so real and so genuine that anyone with an ounce of decency and intelligence would make that connection and would rather talk to her than to me. In the prospect's mind, I am a professional liar. Norma, on the other hand, is perceived incapable of lying. Clients would open up to her like they were long lost sisters and brothers. Norma would leave that office so pumped up because she made a sales call that produced results, and she could not wait to go back and tell others what she did. Talk about a confidence booster.

Let's do the math again, 800 sales calls in four days. Let's assume only 25 percent of the calls will generate business. That's 200 people spending money on your product or service. All of the leads you made contact with were using someone else to fulfill their needs. If those people then bought your product or service, you are stealing business and it is good. ▪

Chapter V: Sex Sells

OK, this one is really out there. But take some time to let it filter—like I had to do the first time it hit me square in the face.

I got a call from someone who said he was a big time developer of hotels, and commercial and retail space. He told me that before I got too impressed with his hot shot big-time-developer credentials that he lost a million dollars last year in his hotel and obviously needed help. Was I interested in helping? I liked this guy.

He had a limo pick me up at the airport. Did I tell you I like this guy?

As the limo drove up to this four star wanna-be five-star hotel, he was waiting for me at the door—outside the door, in fact.

I shook his hand, we exchanged pleasantries, and I got my luggage. We both went through the front doors, and he immediately asked me to put my luggage down and tell him instantly what was wrong with the place.

I saw a lot of marble, mahogany, and artwork. I saw crystal chandeliers. I heard fine music, and I smelled some fine dining. What struck me in the first 15 seconds was that the hotel may have been a little overstated for a major college town market, so that was what I told him. He swiftly told me, "No, that's not it. Guess again."

Now the challenge was on. I continued to look, and I saw two gentlemen standing behind the front desk with their hands clasped behind their backs. They were standing at attention, and dressed in grey tuxedos with long tails and ascots. I went back to the idea that it was a little overstated for the market. "Nope, that's not it. Guess again," he said.

I responded, "Alright, I give up. Why don't you tell me what it is that I'm not seeing?"

He said, "I have two gentlemen standing at the front desk." I said, "Yeeeeessssss," thinking that it may be a trick question. He continued, "I have two gentlemen standing at the front desk, and everyone knows that checking into a hotel should be a sexual experience."

Now, I've checked in thousands of guests. I've spent many, many hours with some of the finest hoteliers in the business. Never once had this thought or comment ever come up before. I know this guy was rambling on and on about something to back up his announcement but I was lost in a couple of thoughts:

- Is this guy right, and I've been clueless for this long?

- This may be a short-lived gig because this guy may be from a different planet.

- I think this guy is a nut job, but I like that the fact that he is getting me to think harder than I have in a while. This guy will be a challenge, and I like challenges.

So, my conclusion after that six-month consulting relationship reduced his "sexual experience" claim to something like the following: checking into a hotel is not and never should be a sexual experience, but it certainly is a concept that pushes personality partnering to the forefront.

Remember the personality partnering bit I gave you in chapter four? At various hotels, I looked for and now saw the guys that pulled up in their red Corvettes wearing Gucci loafers minus the socks (Do you know the personality type yet?) who would almost automatically gravitate to the good looking female. In the absence of a female, they would approach the fun looking dude if they had to choose between an Ego/Expressive or a Stable/Analytic appearance. It's not exactly sex, but comfort level. People will approach others they see as like themselves or someone with a complimentary personality when given a choice. So for fun, I'd stand behind the front desk with my staff. We would see some goobers walk in, and I'd say to the pair of folks we had working the desk, "Bet you a buck he goes up to you Marvin." We would all get a good laugh out of this wagering. I'm just kidding. I never made fun of our guests. OK, yes I did. But I still loved them all and made sure we all busted butt to make them happy.

Booking Bogus Business

You won't read stories about me, or anyone else I know, going through the competition's garbage or getting hired as custodians so we could rifle through files and memos. I'll save that stuff for the movies, but of all the stories in this book, this next one probably comes as close to those movie scenes as any. If someone told me that this next story would also be committing a crime, I would not be surprised. So why am I sharing the story? I want you to consider that someone may have done, or is currently doing, this to you.

I have never done what I am about to describe, mainly because I never thought of it. I heard about it recently, even though it happened a very long time ago. When it happened, I am almost certain it would not have been defined as illegal, but surely would have pushed the concept of ethical theft to its limits. It is easy for me to mentally substitute a steel company or a florist in place of the hotel examples I use, and I suggest you do the same for your business.

There were several major hotels in a big market that would compete head-to-head and toe-to-toe on every piece of business. One hotel was newer, better, and quoted lower rates than the other. Let's call that one Hotel A. You and I are selling for Hotel B.

The convention and visitors bureau (CVB) is a government entity that is paid to bring conventions and other major events into its city. Every major city and many secondary markets have a CVB. These organizations send out leads whenever they get them and all the hotels receive the leads at about the same time.

Working on the premise that the early bird gets the worm, Hotels A and B are all over these leads—calling potential decision makers and trying to get the edge any way they can.

You and I working in Hotel B know that Hotel A will probably quote $100 per guest room per night, so we have to stay close to that rate but preferably lower. We are not as nice as Hotel A, and we really need this business.

We go to our boss, the general manager, and make our case. Our general manager, being the tuned-in and motivating sort, tells us that he is paying us good money to go the extra mile, and we better start pulling our weight. The lowest we can go, he says, is $115 per night. We tell him the client will book at Hotel A. He tells us to get out and go sell something for a change.

We can't go against his wishes, and we really need this business. We also know that we won't get it unless we go to drastic measures.

We close and lock our office door. We ask a friend to call up Hotel A pretending to be a large, potential client needing rooms during the same time period as the CVB lead. Furthermore, we get our friend to make it clear to Hotel A that price is no concern—our friend wants the best of everything. This is a tentative booking. Nothing is definite which means the potential client (our friend) has signed nothing and made it clear that he is just considering Hotel A. That is probably not how Hotel A's team members heard it. They think they have this terrific opportunity to cash in.

This now gets Hotel A to quote a much higher rate than the $100 it has historically quoted. They propose to the CVB lead a $125 per room, per night rate because they are basing their room rate on availability. They can book smaller pieces of business between now and the dates in question, along with our friend's piece of business, and maximize revenue that week.

The CVB client decides to confirm at Hotel B. In the eyes of our general manager, we pulled our weight and sold something (and who would expect it all the time now).

We call up our friend and have him release the dates while explaining to Hotel A that he is going to a different city with his business. That's pretty nasty, huh?

Let's go back a little here and see how much we should have learned from this story. I am not recommending you ever use this tactic, but be aware that it could be happening to you and take steps to protect yourself against it.

Hotel A should have called up our friend and told him that it had a request for the same dates. They should have asked if our friend was going to go from a tentative booking to a definite one. At that time, our friend would have been required to sign contracts or agreements that would bind him to pay for his convention. Obviously, confronted with this question, the jig would have been up and our friend would have disappeared as quickly as he appeared. Hotel A messed up, but that does not justify the actions of Hotel B. So, if you have multiple orders for product or services over the same period of time, or you have to choose one client over another, make sure you choose the business that is going to be definite—not what appears to be the biggest or most valuable.

Emotional Hookers

This story started out as a stroke of luck for me, but then developed into a broader look at how important it is to get clients to realize an emotional connection to my product and service.

At the time, I was the sales director working at a very important hotel for my entire brand. We were a convention center hotel, and it was expected that our revenues and profits would lead the company. It was a great hotel and I had a great sales staff, so we had a lot of fun. The problem was that we were booking a ton of business through the sales office, but we were still missing budgeted projections. I guess we could have sat around in meetings and tried to justify our performance against an unfair budget, but I figured our energies were better spent trying to do more and do better.

We uncovered a major piece of business occurring at a hotel not as nice as ours, but that location was charging a lot less too. We needed to find out if this value-conscious decision maker saw enough benefits in our product and service to warrant paying a lot more money.

After several meetings and tours of my hotel over the course of five months, the client concluded that he could not justify the added investment necessary to doing business with me.

I really wanted that business and was sorry that I couldn't get him to see how much better my property was for his employees and clients. As I was regrouping on how to go back to him with the proof he needed, I got a phone call from him asking to see me right away.

I went over to his office to negotiate a little, and within hours, we agreed to a contract that we both felt very good about. After he signed, he asked me if I wanted to know what it took to finally convince him. I told him that I have no doubt that it was my charm, charisma and intellect. To this, he responded with a hearty chortle causing stuff to come out of his nose and mouth at the same time.

After he composed himself, he told me in these exact

words, "Don, I was riding up the elevator of the hotel we used for more than five years yesterday, and I was propositioned by a prostitute." I was genuinely amazed because in all my years of being in the hotel business, I have only seen one such character. I blurted out something charming, intelligent and charismatic like, "You mean a hooker?" He went on to tell me that he could not in good conscious ask his employees and customers to stay somewhere that would make them feel as uncomfortable as he felt yesterday.

This client made an emotional decision to change hotels, but justified it with reasoning instead of just making a logical decision that felt good. From that day forward, I worked as hard at getting that emotional connection as I did the logical one.

Did I steal this business or did the client mess up? Was it just lucky timing because I had already paved the road over to my hotel? It was a combination of all the above, so never say never. Be selling even before your competition messes up because the vast majority will slip at some point. If you mess up, fess up, and fix it fast. ■

Chapter VI: Creating Loyal Customers

In the Flight Path

There were some airline crews staying at a better hotel than mine—business that I wanted.

The client was very sharp. He would sit in his office in New York and would call me up to ask what I was bidding for his considerable business. He would hang up; call up this better hotel; and tell him what I proposed. That better hotel would counter.

By the third phone call to both of us over the course of a few days, it was clear that he was playing us against one another. All this did was get my competitor to discount the business even further, and I would wind up with nothing.

The general manager from the better hotel called me up and told me that he would do whatever it took to keep that account, so I might as well give up now. That phone call made it personal, so I decided not to give up the chase.

I believed he would match whatever best offer I could produce, so I had to find something he could not offer. This was a better branded hotel with facilities equal to or better than mine in some areas. The general manager was a good communicator and would not be someone I could "out-relationship" with the client.

I put some cards on the table that I didn't realize would be the hand I would have to play. I asked the client if he would take a face-to-face meeting with me at his office in New York City and he agreed to a date.

This gentleman made crew housing decisions all over the country and only personally visited the top markets in which they were spending millions of dollars. He had been to my city a few months prior to my arrival. Therefore, he didn't know we were an option and hadn't seen my hotel.

I took pictures every 25 feet or so, showing him what his crew would experience with my hotel from the time they jumped in our van at the airport, to the lobby, to the sleeping room, to the health club, to the dining room, and back to the lobby, van and airport.

I'm no photographer. I normally have to take 10 shots to get a good one, but on one of the exterior shots of my hotel, you could see the competitive hotel he was using in the background. What I had failed to predict was the reaction this decision maker would have to that one shot.

It showed a DC 10 coming in for a landing, and the way the picture was taken, made it look like the plane was 50 feet from hitting the top of the competition's hotel roof.

The incredulous look on his face was worth a thousand words as he commented that he did not realize the hotel in which he was housing his crews was in a direct flight path. Frankly, I was amazed that this would bother him. Wasn't he in the airline business, and wasn't he indirectly responsible for airplane noise?

This is like when you go to a smaller town, and you smell stuff in the air, and the locals ask if you can identify the smell. Then regardless of your answer, they respond with, "That's money." I guess I thought of airplane noise as being something of which the airlines would be proud.

He asked me if I knew what side of the hotel my competition housed his crews. I told him that he needed to speak up a little because I think I lost some of my hearing standing in front of my competition's hotel that day.

I was able to secure this business that day because I

showed up in his office with one of the best photos I had ever taken. He concluded, with little help from me, that his current hotel was in the flight pattern of major flights during the hours his crews were expected to be sleeping.

You know how some cameras offer a date and time stamp. Well, I had tried to get that feature to turn off and could not figure out how to do it, so the date and time was printed on each picture. He noted the time. This decision maker did not want the hassle of taking union complaints about noise—a painful process for him. He felt he would be proactive before the complaints started coming.

As I arrived back in my office, I played a voicemail from one very irate competitive general manager telling me that I was the lowest form of life on the planet. He couldn't believe how low I was I willing to stoop to steal his business. He stated that my hotel was in the same flight pattern as his and some other choice remarks. The truth is that I am rarely as smart or as stupid as people make me out to be, and he gave me far too much credit for that theft.

How ironic, an airline crew moves hotels because of the airplane noise. You'll be happy to know that I turned a headhunter onto this general manager, and I'm not certain it was my connection, but that general manager got a better job in another city not long after our flight path discussion.

I love competition. It keeps us sharp. But revenge can be one heck of a selling motivator, and I had enough competition without having him single me out as his target.

Overstated Product

Using the emotional buying power that I saw demonstrated in the "Hookers" section, I was "loaded for bear" on this next theft.

This was another situation where a competitor of mine had a much better physical location. The hotel had a large contract where it would house mechanic types who specialized in car alignments.

These mechanics were really the employees of customers who bought the alignment equipment, and the alignment company thought it would be fitting to house them at one of the best hotels in the area. The executives of the alignment company were practicing the Golden Rule—do unto others as you would have them do unto you. They should have been practicing the Platinum Rule.

These mechanics would start their week on Sunday night with a pretty grand dinner and conclude with a ceremony late Friday night.

Before I made my initial sales call, I hung around the lobby and in the dining room watching how these mechanics would interact and what facilities they would use at the competitive hotel (my homework).

After a couple of hours of this surveillance, I could see that there was an emotional disconnect between the product and the mechanics. They looked like school boys dressed up and fidgeting at church. They wanted to be themselves, but they were surrounded by ritz, glitz, and suits. I had to rescue these poor guys. My guess is that some of these folks had never flown before, never heard of beef Wellington, and certainly never stayed in a hotel as nice as the one in which they found themselves.

I made an appointment to see the decision maker at the alignment company, but he made it clear in our initial phone call that he is very happy with his current hotel and is only seeing me out of courtesy.

I shared my little social study with the decision maker and only got him to agree to do one thing for me. I asked him to pass out a survey questionnaire that I developed and his company massaged. It asked how comfortable these employees were with their accommodations. So on Friday evening, they had the ceremony attendees complete the survey.

Early the next week, I followed up with a phone call to hear the results. The decision maker wouldn't tell me the results, but wanted to meet for lunch, so I figured we were in full-negotiation mode at that point.

We did a trial hotel stay with a group two weeks later that the competition did not know we were doing. The attendees loved our more relaxed atmosphere, and it did not hurt that we approached and catered to these guests, as opposed to the competition, that waited for the guest to approach its staff.

We scored that business because of the emotional and logical fit—in that order.

After the trial stay and a full day of negotiating the details, we came to an agreement. The alignment company wanted me to come back in a few days to have a formal signing ceremony with its chief executive officer (CEO), whom I had not yet met. I told the company that I would bring my boss, the general manager of the hotel, too.

At the ceremony we toasted each other with champagne and they had a photographer there who was getting ready to shoot some shots of the signing.

My general manager at the time, who I loved dearly, was from the deep South and with his fine Southern drawl stopped the room dead with four words. He said to the CEO, "I have an idear. Bafah we get to sinon this here agreement, I'd lak to say that there may be a way fah y'all ta save a lil bit mah money." He went on to recommend that instead of our hotel going to the pains of billing the alignment company after each visit that it would save the company money if we billed just once a month. The CEO asked how much they could save.

I got a look from the "generals" with which I negotiated. I couldn't figure if that death stare was because I hadn't made the recommendation or if they were mad at themselves for not thinking of it. They may have just been mad because we had a done deal and now these two leaders were going to muck up the situation.

My general manager threw out a figure that sure seemed to come from the hip. He said he could save the alignment company about $50,000 a year.

It's my turn to talk (I said to myself). "Uh, Gomer (that was not really his name), are you sure you want to do that?" He looked at me and said, "Of course I do." I was forced to say right in front of the alignment brain trust, "Do we really want to wait to get paid?" I went on to say that the time it would take to do the accounting each week was about eight man  hours, and eight man hours times 12 months was a lot less than $50,000 a year. At this point, the "generals" from the alignment company came to my rescue and said they really wanted billing after each visit anyway. Whew!

I never did talk with my alignment contacts about that little exchange, nor did my general manager and I speak of it. I chalked it up to my mistake of not getting him more involved in the actual negotiation. So with future contract negotiations, Gomer was part of the process. He brought a lot to the table, and I should have included him sooner.

Reader Boards

Getting a better understanding of the clients that are currently utilizing the products or services of your competition is a good thing for you.

I would go into a hotel and review the activities for the day posted on the reader board. If there was a company that I did not recognize, I would see what meeting room(s) it was using. If the company was not using meeting rooms, but was staying there, I would go up to the front desk and tell the agent that I had a dear friend who owned that company. I would ask the agent for the name of the person in charge because I wanted to see if my friend was there. I would wind up with a new company name and a contact. Now I would have to dig and find out the rest of the contact data, but that was the easy part.

If the company was meeting in the hotel, I would go to that area and pick up literature that was sometimes left on the registration table outside the meeting room. If it was the end of the day, and the meeting wrapped up, I would also pick up any materials that were left behind.

Sometimes, if I happened to arrive at the same time the group was having a coffee break, I would observe who I felt was most approachable and say, "Excuse me. Could you please tell me who is in charge of booking this group?" They would point someone out to me. If I was "feeling my oats" that day, I would walk up to that person and say, "This certainly may not be the best time to be approaching you, but here is my card. I have a phenomenal hotel close to this location and would really love to host your next meeting. Who is the right person for me to follow up with next week?"

The stunned look on their faces was always precious. If it was a sales meeting that I interrupted, I could almost guarantee you that this exchange would make it into the presenter's hands, and he would announce it to the audience as something they too should be doing in their own industry.

Once in a while, my activities would become known to the sales office of my competition who would offer to send me function sheets every week if I agreed to stay out of their hotel. Legally, the hotel could not stop me from entering or talking to clients, but I would take those salespeople up on their offer and check periodically to make sure they did not eliminate anything from these sheets. Amazingly, they never did withhold information.

I am sure this tactic turned off some potential clients, but the majority was at least curious to find out if I was crazy, desperate or just confident in my product and service. During the follow-up process, it was easy to prove that it was pure pride that drove me to hunt down business in that manner.

Parking Lots

Like reader boards, the parking lots of your competitors can sometimes advertise with whom they are doing business. Often there are trucks and cars that have names of companies or government institutions on them. In the hotel business, there are tour buses. Be sure to check the paper listing on the door and not just the company name on the side of bus.

I've had a client tell me that she would watch for construction crew trucks to stop alongside her car at a traffic light near her hotel. Then, that hotel salesperson would get out of her car, ask the construction crew if they were working in the area, and determine if they needed hotel accommodations.

Many stories like that one have generated business for this client. However, I would advise any woman not to risk her safety by approaching these strangers. You can stay in your car and simply shout at the construction crew through an open window. ▪

Chapter VII: A Fish Too Small

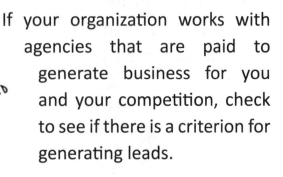

If your organization works with agencies that are paid to generate business for you and your competition, check to see if there is a criterion for generating leads.

In the hotel world, it was already mentioned that we would get convention and visitors bureau leads. Not all CVBs offer this service. But in major cities, these organizations would get a fair amount of calls from people asking for help in finding suitable hotels for their functions. That would amount to smaller pieces of business for hotels. The CVBs had minimum criteria for generating leads that they would then send to all member hotels at least weekly. For those that did not fit this criteria, a "friend" at a hotel would be called directly and asked if they would want to follow up on the lead.

After I discovered this practice, I worked at being the best friend. I would have CVB personnel over for lunches, cocktails, dinners, or for a weekend visit with their families—whatever made sense. You might be thinking that this is not fair, but it is only human to do favors for the people we like best, and those that can help us in return. So get over it, and go make yourself some more friends.

You may even start your relationship building endeavor with the chamber of commerce and visitor information centers. For hotels, these organizations are similar to CVBs except that they may not be sending out printed leads. Instead, they hand out marketing materials or make it easy for your materials to be seen by the public.

The best part about these "smaller fish" leads is that if I lost one, it would not be critical to my hotel's success. Also, because they were smaller, they did not negotiate for big discounts. From a market share, referral opportunity, and risk of loss standpoint, I'd rather have 20 small accounts than one large one.

Use the Competition like a Real Consumer

Get to know the competition firsthand and hear what their front line employees have to say.

Whenever I checked into a competitor's hotel, I would try to do anything and everything I thought a real consumer would do. I would e-mail the hotel from a "neutral" address, not that I thought many would notice an address from the competition anyway. I would see how long it took for an employee to respond and how she worded the response. I would call to make a reservation in order to hear and feel how the consumer was treated. I would make a reservation through the Web site and then cancel to see if the hotel had any marketing in place to encourage me to stay on my next trip or to find out why I cancelled. This first impression stuff told me a lot about what I needed to do to be better with my hotel's first impression.

Regardless if the competition I was researching was primary or secondary competition, I would always be looking for the things it did especially well, as much as I would be looking for the not-so-good moments. I could use both pieces of information to sell and service better.

Every competitor, no matter how messed up they may have been, did at least one thing really well. And 99 percent of the time, I wouldn't say bad things about my competition to a client or prospective client. I tried to show some class and point out when my competition did a good job. During the other one percent of the time, I may have said something bad, but only because the client asked for my input, and I was very good friends with that client. And even then, I watched what I said.

Go to the lounge and start a conversation with the bartender about how busy it is. Ask if they are always this busy, and you will get a host of answers. Some that I recall go like this:

- "Yeah, we get busy every Friday night and you'd think they would schedule more than one bartender."

- "Oh yeah, this is the night XYZ group meets at our hotel. It is here every month." We would then talk about that group and all the particulars that go into taking care of it.

I might have even more fun by telling the bartender that I sometimes go to Hotel B (my hotel) to see what he or she might have to say about my place. Some bartenders offered interesting tidbits about what their bosses said about Hotel B.

Similar to the lounge conversations, test the restaurant or housekeeping staff. Order more towels and see what they say, how they say it, and how long it takes to receive the towels. Unscrew the antenna out of the back of the TV and call the front desk to report that the TV won't work. Find out if the engineering and maintenance staff is responsive. "Kick the tires" in every department you could possible encounter.

I would assemble notes from my weekend stays and make a presentation to the sales staff on my findings. I would take the stuff that the competition did especially well to my general manager and fellow department heads to make certain our hotel could exceed expectations. In areas where we could not exceed what the competition offered, we would find alternatives or at least know what to say if a potential client were to bring up the issue.

Every quarter, I would schedule a visit with my competition, and I would bring as many reservations, front desk and sales staff as possible. This announced visit was to learn more about our competition's hotels. In the event we were full, or could not accommodate a guest's request, we would be able to refer this business to our competitors.

After we would finish this 45-minute tour of each hotel, we would assemble in a van or outside of the hotel where we could not be heard. I would quiz the group on what they heard and saw. I wanted their impressions of weak and strong points. This personal visit by my front line staff would go a long way toward convincing them that we were worth the money we charged. Most of my employees that would take reservation requests had never spent their own personal money on a hotel room that was as expensive as the ones we were asking them to quote. So to get their hearts into their heads and then have the right words come out of their mouths, I needed for them to see, feel, and hear how we compared to the competition.

They still may not spend that kind of money on their own hotel room, but they sure felt better knowing that there are many people that could, would, and most importantly, should at our hotel.

Once or twice a year I would "treat" our head housekeeper or chief engineer by paying for their families to stay at a competing hotel. My selfish return on investment was  that I expected them to come back with what they saw, heard and felt, and based on their experience, how they thought we should raise our standards. This non-typical view of the competition produced some very "out of the box" thinking. Following are a few examples:

- One engineer came back with this notion that we should shut our successful gourmet seafood restaurant, and in its place, build a country and western bar. Why? It was because he loved country and western, for starters. We would have a pretty good laugh about some of these suggestions, but they sure made you think. None of us would have come up with the country and western bar idea on our own.

- A head housekeeper came back and told us how the stay at the competitor's hotel helped her figure out why she was having a tough time getting her room attendants (maids) to show up for work on weekends and why they were so tired during the week. She assumed it was because they had too much fun over the weekend and seemed to be constantly preaching about this to her staff. She found out that they were working at this competing hotel for more money on weekends only. She saw them because they came to clean her room. Imagine everyone's surprise. These room attendants would work for her five days a week and put in another two days on weekends with the competition. No wonder they were so tired. She did a lot of things differently after this encounter. She started having a meeting with her entire staff to get their input on how they could make the money they needed and still get to take one day off a week, if not two.

Another benefit in sending chief engineers and head housekeepers to stay with your competition is that they looked for and found things that typical salespeople and other management would not have seen—like how the competition organized their housekeeping and maintenance carts to maximize efficiencies and reduce labor; which supplies were used that might be better and less expensive; or the number of towels put in the bathroom.

Vampire Feeding

A night audit shift refers to the charming men and women who typically work from 11 p.m. to 7 a.m. at the front desk of a hotel. Their major function is to work on accounting functions that transpired that day; act as night manager for smaller and medium-sized hotels; and oh yeah, check in the very few guests that show up at 2 a.m. You have to be a certain kind of person to like these hours and like this job. Night auditors are typically very Stable/Analytic, which means they are resistant to change and absolutely make decisions from their heads, not their hearts (some don't have one).

The best thing about night auditors from my perspective was that they were often neglected and taken for granted. I delighted then, and still do, at going into a competing hotel to visit with the night auditor. I would tell that person that I was the sales director from my hotel and I could use his help with referrals. I explained that when his hotel was full, people would be walking in or phoning to see if rooms were available that night. I asked for all those referrals.

Now at most hotels, these referrals might only equal one to three rooms a night, but when we would take this approach at 10 hotels, the numbers got to be pretty big and the night auditors became much more important to me.

At my hotel, we would have a monthly breakfast starting at 7:20 a.m. We would get the night auditors to stop by before going home. We would thank them by buying a terrific breakfast, and giving them a tour and a gift before they left.

After the first monthly breakfast, my night auditors were asked to communicate nightly with each of the competing night auditors to make sure we were getting their referrals and to swap ideas on how to do a better job.

Yeah right, these folks were probably hacking into Fort Knox and transferring funds to their Swiss bank accounts, but as long as they referred business to me, that was OK.

Just for a few laughs, I would ask these night auditors

the last time they saw their general manager or one of their own salespeople. You would hear things like, "I saw the back of his head once in 1977." I also heard many accounts from my night auditors telling me that more than a few of their counterparts would send us referrals before filling up their own hotel because we appreciated them more than their own company.

Overflow

Similar to the night audit situation that you just read about, some of our competing hotels would be full by 7 p.m. and they would still be getting calls or guests walking in to find hotel accommodations for that night.

The B shift at a hotel front desk typically worked from 3-11 p.m., so these personnel were an important market segment for us to cultivate.

We already talked about getting my front desk to tour the competition in groups, so that was an opportunity for those employees to meet other front desk people. So when my B shift staff would call into the competition, they had a better connection.

My sales staff would hand deliver full pizzas or six-foot sub sandwiches to the competition earlier during the day because we knew that they would be filling up and we needed them to refer out hotel. The food was a good reminder that we should be the only hotel they recommended, and it worked.

Even if we were not looking for overflow or referral business, we would call our primary competition daily and find out how many rooms they had to sell. In addition, my front desk would call into the competition and pretend to be a potential guest to hear and feel how they sold. My employees would sometimes say that they were considering my hotel and the competitor's hotel, but they were not sure. This would shed light on how the competition fielded those types of calls.

If we ever filled up first or needed to send the competition a guest that wanted something we could not offer, we knew which hotels sent us the most business and could give us the best reciprocal return on investment. That was the hotel that would get our referral. ▪

Chapter VIII: Speak the Language

I got myself on the outside looking in with the owner of a hotel management company for which I was the vice president of sales. This company demoted me to be the sales director for one fairly frumpy hotel. My wife was pregnant with our first child, and I had bills to pay, so the vice president of human resources was able to talk me out of quitting. He told me to prove myself. If I could turn this hotel's revenues around, I could come back as the vice president of sales.

The hotel was decent, physically, but it was off the beaten path in a neighborhood that was only famous for being the home of a couple major car dealerships in the city of Memphis. Memphis is famous for its barbecue; being the home of the blues; and being the leader in shipping cargo. It was not located near the blues entertainment area, and not many people jump on an airplane to spend the night eating barbecue, buying cars and shipping out of the city. This neighborhood didn't do much for my hotel's potential to increase revenues. I was in Memphis' version of southern Siberia.

The biggest companies in Memphis at the time were Fed Ex and Holiday Inns, which moved to Atlanta with pieces of the company moving to London. That left only Fed Ex. International Paper moved its headquarters to Memphis, but that came later. So, how does one sell a hotel to this kind of a market?

My solution was to sell the hotel to Fed Ex. Not just for sleeping rooms, meeting and banquets, but to sell them the bricks and mortar—turning the whole building into a training facility. Fed Ex was using some really nice hotels all over the city for various training events and for crew housing for folks not based in Memphis. I did not know exactly what they were spending, but I guessed. I figured Fed Ex could save money and control the quality of the facility if it owned its own hotel.

The general manager and I became very good friends and we were really enjoying making inroads into different Fed Ex departments with some success. We were employing many of the tactics you are reading in this book, so we were doing better financially. But the one thing that got me back into the good graces of the owner was sending Fred Smith, CEO of Fed Ex, a note.

In this note, I spelled out why purchasing the hotel for Fed Ex's own usage made terrific sense. I don't think the note got to Fred, but I did receive a reply from a senior official of some kind. The reason I received a response wasn't because my idea to have the company buy the hotel was so revolutionary. It was because I sent the note to Fed Ex in a Fed Ex envelope that got people's attention—my boss's boss and even that of senior executives inside Fed Ex. I'm sure the package sorting was done electronically, but I had fun drawing up a mental picture of this Fed Ex employee at the central "hub." When she picked up my package from the Memphis origination bin only to see that it was staying in Memphis, she must have thought I had a lot of money to burn by not sending it U.S. mail, by courier, or delivering it myself.

So I learned firsthand how powerful your message can be when you use the product and services of potential clients to communicate to them. It would be like sending Teleflora flowers to Teleflora and telling them I wanted to do business with the company. How about buying a corned beef sandwich from a deli courier and having it delivered to the deli with a note explaining that you wanted to be the deli's mustard provider? There are a lot of examples that fit here.

I know you want to know what happened with me in that job don't you? Six months or so after being demoted to the frumpy hotel, the owner and my immediate boss wanted me back as the vice president of sales. They told me I was a genius for sending Fred that note via Fed Ex; how things were going to be greater than they were before; and how they missed me—blah, blah, blah. I quit that very day and started my consulting company, which later became the world's largest training company. My partner in this business venture was the general manager that I befriended at the frumpy hotel. Things happen for a reason. Is it fate?

The truth is, I should have been in trouble or fired for the many stunts I pulled in my selling lifetime, but I rarely did these stunts to gain a greater position or more money for myself. I did them because I thought they were the best things for the hotel I represented.

Be All Things to Everyone

This statement surely flies in the face of professional advice you would receive from the vast majority of highly paid consultants in the business world. They would tell you to stay focused on your primary skills—do what you do best. I have a little different twist on things.

When I did consulting 100 percent of the time (1986-1990), I guaranteed hotel owners and operators that with my help they would make a certain amount of money in a set period of time. If I failed, they paid me nothing, so what was my secret? I used the tactics you are reading about in this book.

In every single case, I would ask the general manager and sales director of the hotel for which I was working how many market segments they were pursuing. They would typically say six to nine. I would triple the amount of market segments that they should, could, and would be pursuing.

I once did consulting work for a hotel that was losing a million dollars a year. The reservations manager, a staff of one, was hanging up on 20 calls every few minutes because, according to her, the property was not near the beach and that is what callers were asking. Not only did we find a positive way to say where the hotel was located, we also became all things to all people or at least a lot of things to a lot of people.

As an example, if someone called that hotel and asked if we had a honeymoon suite, we would respond, "We don't have a suite, but we have a real cool honeymoon package complete with his and her pajamas that you can take home with you and all the fixings for a pillow fight." The next call would come into the reservation office and the caller would want to know if we had bird-watching packages. Our reservations personnel, now a staff of two, would ask "Do you mean like real birds, and you sit outside and hunt them with binoculars?" The caller would be a little cautious at this point and say, "Uhh yeah, real birds." This would get a hearty, "Of course we have bird-watching packages," from our end, and we would be constructing a package right on the spot. Do you have a Valentine's Day package? Yep. A honeymoon package? Of course we do.

The more diversified we were, the more it opened up employees' minds to what we offered. At that point, all we had to do was construct sales action plans that targeted the consumers who "fit" into those market segments. Following the plan, we would make sales calls with the right value proposition that was customized specifically for the prospect's needs.

In essence, we were stealing business from those competitors whose brands focused on a few targeted market segments. We stole from those that thought they were big fish in a small pond. We stole from anyone. You might say we were equal opportunity thieves. We did not discriminate against anyone from which we could steal business.

Targeting Winners

I do not recommend that you do this, but be aware that others have and will continue this practice.

I was the vice president of sales for a hotel management company and visiting an under-performing hotel in our portfolio. I spent a morning with the general manager on those things he was doing to increase revenues. He had a lot in the pipeline. He just needed to close more deals.

We agreed that we needed to pull all of these potential customers into the same room together and get them to buy in a great big wave of revenues for this hotel. How to best do this—like in Animal House—was with a party that everyone would be up for.

We had the sales office conduct a phone blitz inviting the top potential accounts and the best existing accounts. We wanted happy clients at the party talking to potential clients and serving as third-party recommendations. The general manager and I went out and made a bunch of personal cold calls on the bigger accounts to make sure they would show up.

On one of the larger potential sales calls, this general manager asked the decision make if she would come to the party. She said something like she would try, but that she wasn't sure. The general manager said to her that we were giving away some very cool prizes like trips to Hawaii and so on. She got all excited and said it had been a lifelong dream of hers to go to Hawaii, to which the general manager responded, "I think you will win, but you have to come to the party."

The night of the reception, we were conducting tours and soft selling to the potential accounts. When the attendees entered the room, they received numbered tickets for the drawings and prizes.

The general manager personally handed out the tickets wishing good luck to all on winning the trip to Hawaii. The woman who we met earlier, whose dream it was to win, was in attendance. The general manager told his

sales director to palm the ticket, so that when she went in to the bowl to draw a winner, this large potential account would miraculously win. The sales director wanted nothing to do with this, so the general manager asked me to do it. "No way," I said. He ended up doing it himself, and after he announced the winning ticket number, this woman yelled at the top of her lungs, "I can't believe it. When you came to see me earlier today and said I would win, I just did not believe you. I can't believe my luck!"

Being the quick thinker that he was, the general manager reassured the now lynch-forming audience that he told everyone on the way into the banquet room that he thought they would win. He really did.

We had more than a few folks who thought this was a big fix, but after a few more free cocktails and free food, everyone had a grand time. I know we booked a lot of business that night, but I distinctly remember that this woman went on her all-expense-paid, Hawaiian vacation and never did book a single thing with our hotel. She was as dumb as dirt, and did not know there was an expected return on investment to her trip.

The lesson learned: It is OK to steal, but not cheat.

Eastern Onion

It almost always felt like I would share a selling formula with someone, and the next opportunity they would face would be out of the norm.

Eastern Onion is just one of the services that provided singing telegrams and other announcements done in a fun way. If I had a potential client that would not take my calls, answer e-mails or agree to see me, I would send over a parade of gifts and attention getters until they caved. You can't create loyalty if you can't get them to talk to you.

The potential of a particular client or the severity of the situation (we messed something up and lost the account) would determine how often I would send stuff over to the potential client's office. Flowers on Monday with a note; a pie delivered on Wednesday with a note; balloons on Friday with a note, and so on.

I'll share something someone did to me to get my attention. I was a regional sales director at the time and was responsible for the advertising monies for about 40 hotels. I had this small ad agency calling me, and while I usually returned all calls even if it was to tell the caller I would not use his services, I just ignored this company's phone calls and the marketing pieces they mailed to me.

After numerous failed attempts to reach me, this agency sent over a courier with a square box that measured eight inches by eight inches and the first thing you noticed was that it had holes on the top. So my administrator signed for the box and does what anyone would do. She shook it to hear if anything jingled. No jingling, but there was definitely something alive in this box. She shrieked and dropped the box on her desk causing a commotion that got the attention of everyone in the office. At this point, an army of office personnel squeeze into my office requesting I open the box, so that they could see what was in it.

First, I opened the note attached to the outside of the box, and it said something to the effect that the agency had tried to reach me, and because I was so busy, they thought they would try this approach. The note asked me to please open the box and send my reply using the enclosed tiny return note.

I was too chicken to open it, so my administrator did it for me. Inside was a carrier pigeon with a capsule attached to its leg. The little note had two questions on it. I was supposed to check one of two boxes. Box one said, "Yes. I want you to call me and set up a meeting," and the second box said, "Don't bother me again." I opted to create a third box for which I wrote, "I don't want to see you, but I sure would like to know where you got the carrier pigeon." I rolled up the note and my administrator stuck it the pigeon's capsule. She carried it outside with the entire office in tow to see what would happen. Someone smarter than me calculated the direction of the ad agency, and we wanted to see if the pigeon knew its way home. She let the bird go and it does a complete, 360 degree circle high above us and then headed in the direction of the agency.

Talk about an attention-getter. Not only did the agency get me to notice it, but 40 or so other people from my office noticed. I did finally agree to meet with the agency, and unfortunately, it was too small to handle our needs. This goes to show that big ideas can come from small companies.

The last story in this chapter is related to getting someone's attention, but not for "selling" purposes. Early in my consulting practice, I did some really good work for a client who ran up a big bill with me. He then promptly filed for bankruptcy. I had over $25,000 in expenses that I owed American Express. I was going to be in a world of hurt if he did not pay me at least the expenses he owed. I composed a poem— humorous but clear—about expecting to get paid. I called his office and found out that he was in the building, so I hired Eastern Onion. I sent someone over to his office, dressed in a gorilla costume, and had that person read my poem. All the planets must have been aligned that day because three things came together in one fell swoop.

As luck would have it, the receptionist interrupted a meeting he was having with lawyers, bankers and a few investors who were considering buying into his company to pull him out of his financial woes.

She wanted to know if he wanted the gorilla to go home or to perform for him. As it turned out, his birthday was approaching and he thought that was the reason for the visit. He dragged the entire meeting into his lobby, along with a bunch of his staff, to see this gorilla read my poem.

I found out later that the guy in the gorilla suit had been wronged by a partner in a previous business dealing and had to take odd jobs to pay off debts—thus the Eastern Onion gig. So this gorilla was delivering "poetic justice" as he gave it his all, belting out my poem.

Later that day, I got a call from this client and he was absolutely furious with me. He threatened to sue, slander, suffocate, and more. You've heard the saying, "When you owe the bank millions, the bank has a problem. When you owe the bank a few thousand, you have a problem." What this client failed to realize was that I had more at risk than he did. I was a one man operation with a, once again, pregnant wife and one- year-old daughter for whom I needed to provide. I called up that client and told him that if I was not paid what I was owed, there would be more deliveries to his office.

I think I wound up getting about a third of what he owed me, and I survived, but I'm not sure he did. I've inquired off and on for years, but nobody knows where he wound up. ▪

Chapter IX : Never Say Never

For those people who have messed up with customers and those customers said they will never return, this story is for you.

First things first, you messed up, so fess up. Let your staff know that you did not create loyalty with this client and you owe him or her. This is good for your culture and makes for some fun times while attempting to get the customer back.

One of the first things I did when I arrived at an existing hotel operation was to ask the entire sales team to bring in all the accounts that were ever lost. I then helped them get these people back to the table to see what could be done to re-earn their business.

On one occasion, my sales manager and I were trying to get a large account that we had lost because we had performed horrifically more than once. The last straw for the account came when, at the company's Christmas party, a few of its employees saw our bartender steal the

purse belonging to the CEO's wife. When they immediately reported it to the hotel manager on duty, our manager said they must have been seeing things because our employees don't steal. In essence, he called the CEO and his employees liars without investigating any further. Those employees were gone, and now it was up to me and the sales manager to get the account back.

The CEO wasn't returning my calls, so I went to his office unannounced. The receptionist said upon my arrival that if I had an ounce of intelligence, I would leave immediately and never come back. I told her I was there to face the consequences, and I appreciated her warning. I asked her to please forward my card to the CEO and see if he would agree to meet with me. She got up and walked about 20 steps to a narrow hallway where she handed my card to a gentleman whose back was toward me and the lobby. He took the card, turned around and yelled out, "Tell Mr. Farrell I am not in," and then proceeded to tear the card up into little pieces. The receptionist returned to me with my card in shreds and said she tried to warn me. The other sales slugs in the lobby waiting to see folks at this company had a good laugh at my expense.

Let the games begin, I thought to myself. We began our balloons, cakes, flowers, and Eastern Onion campaign to get this CEO to call me. On the note, I said all I wanted was a 15-minute, face-to-face meeting to apologize, and if he did that, I would stop sending over the stuff. We sent three shipments a week for about a seven-week period. This was getting expensive and was getting me nowhere. As I was about to give up, I finally got the call from the CEO who is actually laughing at the latest delivery. I believe it was an ant farm with a note that said, "I will stop bugging you if you see me."

He said he would come the following night for one free cocktail, so he would at least get something out of the meeting. My sales manager and I constructed our game plan, which was very simple—throw ourselves on our swords and ask for forgiveness.

He showed up, we ordered cocktails, and I started telling him that we deserved to lose him, but that we wanted another chance to do right. He said, "It won't happen in a million years—no way, no how." He was happy with the hotel that he was currently using.

My sales manager interrupted my next thought with a question. He asked the CEO how much money he spent on his annual meeting. The CEO asked back if he meant everything including limos, entertainment, flights, hotel bill, and the whole "shooting match." My sales manager said yes, everything. At this point, I was wondering where this line of questioning was going. The CEO threw out some astronomical number that resembled my mortgage payment for the rest of my life. Even the CEO is perplexed as to why he would be asking. My guy said, "So if I were to tell you that we would pay for it all, every single thing, would you let us host this annual meeting?"

At this point, I moved my glasses down to the bridge of my nose to get a good last look at the sales manager who used to work for me. The CEO repeated every word my sales manager told him and listed all the things for which we would pay. My sales manager said, "That's right. We will pay for all of that." The CEO responded that he would be a fool not to take us up on that offer. My sales manager said, "Well, we aren't going to do that, but I'm delighted that you would be willing to give us another chance."

The CEO couldn't catch his breath. He started to say something and stopped short only to start another something and stop again. He finally said in desperation, "Look you two. What do you want from me?"

We got that company back one small meeting after another, so it took a long time before he trusted us with everything he had.

Lightning Won't Strike Twice

Here is another case where I had messed up and had to get an unhappy client to come back. Sometimes all the selling formulas and past experiences get thrown out and you have to do and say what comes from the heart. In my very first sales position, I had booked a large association that I forgot to give to the administrator in our catering department. This was before computers, so we had to manually block the client's  meeting and banquet needs into very large books we called diaries. Not blocking the needed space meant that another salesperson would block the space I needed, and we would essentially wind up double booking the same space for the same dates. I sent our agreements that the client signed, so as far as it was concerned, everything was in order. Even with computers, this can happen, but there was probably more room for error during this time. Frankly, I'm surprised that it only happened to me once.

Almost a whole year went by. About 45 days before the

client's function, I got a call. The group must have been wondering why I didn't call to provide updated details. When the association called my office looking for me, I was out on sales calls. At the end of the day, I returned to a mildly panicked catering department wanting to know if I messed up or if the association had the wrong hotel.

When I discovered what I had done, and failed to do, I also saw that there was no more space in my hotel to handle this convention. So I met with my boss, and we scrambled all resources to find another hotel that could handle this convention on such short notice. We found a mediocre hotel (all the good ones were full), and I went to see this association. I had "hat in hand" and was ready to grovel when conveying the bad news and what I was prepared to do to make it right.

Now you are going to think I am making this up, but this was an association of magicians, so I thought I would start our conversation with "A funny thing happened on my way here. The space disappeared," and maybe some other stupid lines that would loosen them up.

On second thought, I decided this was no laughing matter and that I needed to just stay calm, and deliver the news directly and swiftly. My hotel would pay for wine, pay for dessert, help with transportation, send a mailing to all members telling them it was our error, and provide info about the new hotel.

The conference planners for the magicians association were not happy, but they were professional and more courteous than I deserved. I left that meeting setting up a conference call between the new hotel and the association folks to make sure the new place would not miss a beat.

A few days after the magicians held their conference at my competitor's hotel, I asked if I could stop in for a visit. They agreed to a meeting, at which time, I once again apologized. I wanted to find out how the conference went. Although the hotel tried hard, the association gave it a "C" average.

To the association folks' surprise, I asked them if my hotel could host their next annual meeting. Before they could say no, I told them that because I had messed up so badly, my hotel would be taking even better care of them. Besides, I said, "What are the chances that lightening strikes twice in the same spot?" This gave them a pretty good laugh. Sometimes you get lucky and say just the right thing the right way at the right time. We got the business.

Truth is, it was not just the words, but more the act of going to the association offices and admitting my mistake. It is about getting these clients to feel the passion and not just hear the words.

Basic American Value—Come Kick Our Tires

There is something to be said for letting buyers give your product or service a trial run before they decide to buy.

How many times have you bought a set of tires for your car without seeing them, comparing them, feeling them, and even smelling them? How about a toaster or a blow dryer?

Coming up through the hotel ranks doing room service or working as a bellman, I would observe people without reservations walking up to the counter at my four-star hotel and asking to see the room before they paid for it. They would usually be met with a look and response that had every bit of a "you've got to be kidding me" feel to it. Sometimes, the front desk agent would even call the security guard and have them accompany this potential guest. Imagine how that conversation went as they walked to the room. This always bothered me that we did not encourage people see us, try us, or "kick our tires" before they bought.

Many years later, I was checking out a new hotel brand that had popped up in the early 1980s. My brand didn't consider it to be competition. I was always looking for new and better ways to do things, regardless of the industry and whether or not they competed directly with us. I went to the front desk and asked if I could see a room.

The front desk agent told me that I simply had to turn around and go to a room off the lobby that had a velveteen rope across the entrance. You could look into the room and see everything, but you could not enter it. As I am peeking in, I asked the agent if all rooms were in this condition and he said they were. He went on to add that the room I was observing was rented every night of the week except Sundays. The people that developed the brand had already determined that their consumer was one that wanted to see the value before they laid down their hard-earned money. I asked myself why my hotel didn't have that same commitment.

After that experience, I decided to take things a step further. If I had a client who was considering my hotel and my competition's hotel, I would try to gain an advantage by offering a free stay. I would say to potential clients, "Now that we have had a chance to talk about the many benefits of my property, I would like for you to not take my word for it. We would love to have you and/or your family stay with us for a night—even the weekend if that works for you. Please give me 10 or 15 minutes notice when you are coming. It won't cost you a dime, and you can see our customer service firsthand."

These potential customers would typically be surprised at such an offer, and I would venture a guess that 50 percent of the folks to whom I made the offer agreed to work with me right then and there. Only about one in 10 would actually take me up on the offer, but 100 percent of them liked that I made it.

Fill in the Blanks

Many advertising agencies will tell you that one of the secrets to getting potential buyers to buy is to get them to feel as though your product or service will help them regain control of their lives. If you subscribe to this same line of thinking, then you may like what my associates and I would do if our business was forecasted to be especially low for a specific time period.

We would see this downturn in business coming at least 60-90 days ahead of time. In the hotel world, it was usually a holiday period or a season that historically didn't do well because of climate and other factors.

We would have an internal form on which we would communicate what things groups wanted and when they wanted them. We called it a BEO or banquet event order, and it spelled out sleeping room needs, meals, coffee breaks, and even audio visual needs. We would mail this form, attached to a cover letter, in a good-sized envelope to select, existing clients—clients that had used us in the past.

The cover letter would ask them to fill in the blanks regarding any upcoming function for which they would consider using our hotel. We even asked them to put in the price they would want to pay. These clients seemed to always get a kick out of this mailing—like they were seeing a part of our business that they normally didn't see.

More times than not, they would put down a price that was greater than what we would have quoted. For those that had a ridiculously low number, we would call back to clarify. We would say something like, "Our normal rate is $150 a night and you said you wanted to pay $15.

Somewhere between our two numbers is something I know we can agree upon." They would chuckle, and the negotiation would not last long before we got them to pay what we would accept.

The return on investment would look something like the following:

- Mail out or e-mail 1,000 pieces (with permission).

- From the 1,000, we would get 50 forms that were completed and returned.

- From those 50, we would book 20 meetings, banquets and sleeping room groups totaling more $100,000.

My feeling is that we had three kinds of people that would book because of this marketing approach:

- Those that would have normally taken care of their business in-house because it was a low-budget project. They would have used their own meeting room and hired a caterer. Our "white sale" offer would be too tempting to pass up.

- Those that would actually move an event into our desired time table from a later date in order to get the good rates.

- Those that would typically use my hotel for "nicer" events and use my lower-priced competition for smaller-budgeted affairs. They would now move this smaller event into a nicer product for an affordable price.

Back of the House

Lawyers, insurance people and those folks that worry about the "one in a thousand," take cover.

There is something sexy about the hotel business with which people are fascinated. They love seeing, hearing, smelling and feeling the behind-the-scenes action. I know I am the same way when I go on a tour of a brewery, a tractor plant, or even a cigarette manufacturing facility (I don't even smoke). Is there something about your place of business that potential customers would like to see?

Especially when a potential client was considering my hotel, and others, I would make it a point to take him into the kitchen and housekeeping areas, and would especially like to accidentally run into my PM person. PM stands for preventative maintenance, and when done correctly, was an impressive initiative. It included a customized work cart complete with tools and sleeping room stuff like washers, toilet seat bolts, air filters, light bulbs or anything that wears out in a room (except carpet and furniture). A PM person should have a checklist of around a hundred things he examines in a room to see

if those items need replacing *before* they break. In an eight hour shift he may only have time to perform preventative maintenance on three to four rooms a day. Therefore, if you have a 150-room hotel, it would take 40-50 work days to check the entire sleeping room portion of the hotel, and then you start over again—theoretically never stopping.

I would ask a PM person what area of the hotel he would be working in on the days I knew I was going to be touring with prospects. If he was going to be in a remote location, I would ask him if he could move to another area for the morning or afternoon, and the PM person always accommodated me.

Why? It was because as I was touring the hotel with the prospect, I would say with my choreographed surprise, "Oh hey, here is our PM person, George. Let me tell you what he does. Or better yet, why don't you tell Ms. Client what you do." The first time I made this request of George he was taken by surprise, but did a good job anyway. From the second to the 100th time, George could have won an Academy Award. He was that good. The prospect was usually sold right after that chance meeting. Did we cheat? No. Did we lie? No. Did we choreograph? Yes.

From kitchens with big ovens and great smells, to huge dishwashing machines, we would show anything and everything. In the housekeeping area, the potential clients would be blown away at the sheer volume of laundry that we would deal with on a daily basis. I don't need to tell you that the employees and the areas needed to be as clean and hazard free as possible—not just because the guest could probably sue us if she fell or a knife was accidently thrown her way, but for the opportunity to create that lasting impression.

Car dealers take note: It is beyond my understanding why you don't have a glass wall that repair customers can look through to see their cars being serviced; while work is being done on all cars. The only thing I can think of is that you are hiding something. You would rather we "hole up" in some bland reception area smelling of scorched coffee storing old newspapers so we can commiserate with each other on why our cars break down. Think this through car dealers and let us watch your version of HBO through the glass instead of letting us get depressed listening to others moan about your product. I have to believe that you lose more future sales in your own reception area than anywhere else on the planet.

Consultant Who Can Get You the Job You Want

Someone in a position of influence in her company and in her market may be able to make this next example of stealing work. It's going to test your feelings of what is ethical and what is not, so strap on your seat belt.

I would walk up to a competitor's front desk and ask the employee(s) who was in charge of their sales effort.

Then I would walk into the sales office and ask for this person with no appointment. Half the time, I was treated like I had leprosy and was only able to get that sales director's business card. That's when I would call back and schedule an appointment. The other 50 percent of the time, the sales office personnel would do what all of us should do and welcomed me as they would a client—meaning they didn't hate me until they were sure they should.

I would tell this sales director the truth—that I did this all over the country, and in this particular case, was working for the owners of Hotel X. I was visiting key competitors to see if there was any opportunity for networking or a way for us to refer business to one another. I would assure them that if they helped, I would return the favor either professionally or personally. What the recipient of this message heard was that I may have connection that they did not, and I could help them find employment elsewhere. There were a lot of dynamics in play here.

I'd go so far as to say most hotel owners and operators don't know how salespeople think—what motivates them and how to maximize the return on investment with each of them. As a result, there are many unhappy salespeople in the world looking for greener pastures— a selling heaven. They are looking for a place where they can do what they  do best and be compensated fairly for that work. Their personality styles typically have short attention spans where they need "victories" more frequently than, let's say, accountants.

I used this underlying condition to my utmost advantage. I have had a surprising number of sales directors, within 20 minutes of meeting me for the first time, hand me their entire marketing plan complete with best clients contact data. And I promise you, I didn't ask for it. Would

I recommend this sales director to another client? Absolutely not; but that won't stop me from exploiting a competitor who is foolish enough to not foster loyalty because of his absolute disdain for his business. I am not endorsing taking copyrighted drawings or plans from your competition, so let me be clear on that.

The salespeople I would recommend are those who would throw me a bone in the form of business leads when they could not or would not work with that lead. These salespeople would make it clear that those leads were all I was going to get, but that they did want to work with me.

I distinctly remember a day when I first sat down with the president of a management company in a major city, and we somehow began a discussion on how to best manage a salesperson. We got into a fairly heated debate on whether or not to manage a sales force by activity or productivity. I remembered telling him there were ways to manage productivity before the business was closed. He was adamant that they should be managed by activity. It got to the point that I was going to get fired before I even left his office to see the hotels for which he wanted me to make recommendations.

I got to his first hotel and was sitting with the general manager of this large, well-known and respected hotel brand. I asked him how many sales files they were working, and he said six. "Wow, 6,000 files," I said. "That is good." He said, "No, six." I said, "You mean 600?" He said, "No, six."

I found out the hotel was 10 years old. How in the world can you only have six files in a hotel that has been around  that long? That was my next question. He took me into the sales office and showed me the rusted outlines of where three large filing cabinets used to stand. The sales director had asked the maintenance men to wheel them out to her car and load them in her trunk a few days prior.

Can you imagine someone in a Honda Civic driving down the road with the back end scraping the ground from the weight of these filing cabinets?

Did the maintenance men know what was happening? Of course they did. The sales director probably helped them load a boiler or two into their trucks as a return favor.

So I think back to the conversation I had with the president regarding how to best manage salespeople, and I would make a safe guess that he did not manage that activity.

While leaders are debating semantics, their salespeople are working hard on their next job. The bottom line, if you have unhappy salespeople, they will steal from you. In essence, you will have trained your newest competitor. Learn how to manage them while keeping them happy. ■

Chapter X: Let's Make a Deal

There are times and situations where you need to make statements about how crazy you are to be the most successful in your market. The net result will be that your competition will want to be aligned with you and not have to compete against you.

I flew back into my home city and was waiting for my hotel van to pick me up. It was snowing and bitterly cold as I waited for my driver curbside.

What felt like 20 minutes was probably more like 10 because I saw many of my competitors' vans driving past me picking up other passengers. One particular competitor's van had driven past me twice, when on the third pass, he pulled up in front of me and opened the side door. He bet me that I am waiting for the XYZ Hotel van (my hotel), to which I replied, "Yes, I am."

How did he know? He told me there were a lot of people, many waiting as long as I had, and they all had reservations at my hotel. He said I could jump in his warm van, enjoy some hot coffee, and when I got to his place, I could call and cancel my reservations at XYZ Hotel without penalty because it was before 6 p.m. I told him thanks, but no thanks. Now I was furious at my hotel.

My van driver finally showed up without so much as an apology or a warm greeting. He didn't even try and open the door for me, and I am a big tipper especially with my own people.

In the hotel world, when bad weather hit, the airport properties scrambled to pick up rooms from those passengers that couldn't get out of town because of cancelled flights. It was as close to hand-to-hand combat as it gets, and the competitor's driver showed me firsthand that my hotel was losing this battle before we even knew we were in the fight.

I immediately marched into the general manager's office ranting and raving, and all he could do was tell me about the tough phone calls he had been fielding from the corporate offices about our low average rates (an average of all the room rates charged to our guests). So he warned me that I should not get involved in anything that would lower our average rates.

I've already said and implied more than a few times that I have done things for which I could have been fired, but I also knew that he was under pressure to deliver only one metric. The most important metric in this equation was bringing in as much money as we could each and every day. If we failed to bring in the money, it was lost time and space that I could never get back. So, could I be fired? Yes. Should I be fired for doing what I was about to do? No.

I called a meeting with the front desk manager and the best van driver I had, which was Reggie. Both of these people told me that they wanted no part of my scheme to fill up during these "distressed" times when weather created the chaos that it did for airports and airport businesses. I wound up signing one-page documents relieving them of any responsibility if caught. I reminded both of them what Reggie stood to make for himself, his bellman and his van drivers—a lot of tip money. The front desk manager's bonus was tied to revenues, so she stood to do well too. The only guy not on an incentive program (at the time) was me, but that's another story for another time and another book.

So, the next blizzard arrived, and we were in DEFCON 5. Reggie had a full complement of drivers canvassing every terminal of the airport practicing what we trained them to do. We copied the competition's driver and offered passengers stranded at the curb a chance to get to a warm hotel immediately. We asked how much they were paying at the competition, and we would match those rates. The drivers would get their full vans back to the hotel, and in the very back of the lobby. They would put up fingers telling the front desk agent how much the line was going to pay. The agent would write it on the room folio. She would ask the guests if that was the rate they were quoted and the guests would confirm. Keep in mind, different van loads would have different rates.

After a few hours of complete success, a competitor's van pulled up behind one of ours. Now an outright auction was going on right there in the middle of a snow storm at the airport curb. The other guy would yell out $50 and

the crowd would jockey to get in his van. When my guy would say $48, they would then turn to go in my hotel's van. We told the van drivers that they could only go as low as $40. That was working well until the competition quoted $38 and my van came back empty. Reggie told me what happened, and I calculated that we still didn't have enough rooms occupied to fill that night, so we came up with a new strategy.

On the next occasion that my van pulled up behind the competition's van and the auction began, I told the van driver that when the other hotel got to $50 to instantly go to $10. The crowds on the street would be laughing at this exchange and could not believe their good luck because they would have paid more.

What happened next was what we were counting on. Anytime the competition saw our van approaching they would head to the other side of the airport because they knew we were crazy enough to do whatever it took to win. When they went to other side we would get business for $75 a room. By the way, when our vans came back with a few $10-a-night loads, the agent would look at the fingers being held up by the van drivers and was waiting for more fingers than 10 to go up. She was in shock when the van driver signaled that this was all that was being charged.

I figured I had a day or two before the general manager found out what I did, so I went on the offensive. I told him what we had been up to and what to say when the corporate office called about our lower than normal average rate. Our revenues had grown 23 percent, and I reminded the general manager that his bonus was also tied to revenues, not the average rate. I was guessing at this point because I didn't really know his bonus formula, but I must have guessed right because he was fairly pleased with the results. However, he was not pleased with the methods and I received another stern warning in a long line of stern warnings.

Competitors' Egos

Be humble and be stupid, and your competitors will tell you things and do things that will help you steal from them. I may be a better actor than I give myself credit for because I was always good at coming across stupid. I'm kind of a natural talent in that department.

A few examples come to the top of my mind. I was in a Midwest primary market that was especially hard hit by the economy and trucking de-regulation. This market was down somewhere close to 40 percent, so I ordered up a large sales blitz for a week. We brought in many salespeople from my other markets to help us make hundreds of sales calls. In our daily recap meetings, we heard story after story about businesses closing up and companies laying off hundreds of workers who now have no need for hotels. I had never had such poor results from a blitz and was about as bummed as I think I had ever been at an effort that I initiated.

It was the tail end of the week, and I asked my sales director to go to lunch with me at the number one competitor's hotel. On the drive over, she told me that the sales director at her competing hotel was one of her best friends, so I asked her to make sure she invited the sales director to join us. I know what you are thinking. Who needs friends? I would say that we all need friends like the one in the following story.

As we get settled in our dining room booth her friend joined us acting a little more than scattered—the easiest kind of salesperson from whom to get information. I told her that I couldn't believe how tough her market was and how our sales blitz was a total waste of time and money.

I congratulated her on how busy her lobby and restaurant were. I flattered her some more by asking about her secret to success. She then started sharing stories about an account they had at the hotel that was very large, but very hard to please, and she was at her wits end trying to cater to this client's every need.

I agreed with her that if it wasn't for all the people we had to deal with, business would be fun. Yes, I know there is a place in hell for people like me.

We got to my sales director's car after our luncheon, and I asked her what she heard. She started recalling all the dumb things we talked about. As she glanced over to see the incredulous look on my face, she finally got it.

She then told me that she couldn't steal business from her best friend. We then had a healthy discussion about how she didn't need more friends. She needed to provide for her current best friends that worked at her hotel. I asked her how she was going to do that while being unemployed. We immediately went and called on the large and difficult account.

I remembered on several other occasions being invited to grand openings and grand re-openings of competitor hotels. Some invited my sales team and me because they wanted to network with the selling leaders in the market and some did it because they wanted to show off their new wares. What kind of an ego would invite people who could steal business to a room full of his best accounts? Once again, an ego that has run amok.

We would be saying nice things about the competition in discussions with their customers and even with my accounts that showed up for the free cocktails and hors d'oeurves. My clients would often times apologize to me for being there, which I always found funny.

At some point, however, the client or potential client would ask me about the new things that were happening or about to happen at my hotel. I would always be more than happy to share this information with them. I swear we booked more business at my competition's parties than we did at our own.

A new job even found me once when I was circulating and working a banquet room at a competitor's grand re-opening. A corporate vice president of sales wanted to know who the salesperson was that was working the hardest. While other salespeople hung out together, I would be working the clients. He thought I was one of his sales staff and was stunned that I worked for the competition. That was until he hired me away, and I spent the next eight years with that company in different selling capacities.

Alcohol can be a truth serum of sorts. Take your hotel competitors out for a few beers and see what you can learn. Be careful that you are not the one doing all the talking.

Be Memorable

You shouldn't need a name tag. When I stop and think about all the people you and I have met and the many folks who have come and gone, I'm amazed at the number. People are born; they live; and then they die. Often times, we don't even remember their names or what good they did when they were here. It has to be the saddest thing in life to have lived and not be remembered for anything positive.

I know I am a little whacked, but I have a personal aversion for wearing a name tag. I guess my feeling is that if the customer, client, or guest doesn't remember my name, then I need to do a better job of becoming memorable.

Don't live your whole life needing to wear a name tag—be known for something. When you sell and when you serve, have a unique way about you that folks will remember. I would make sales calls with a manager of mine. After walking into an office with a receptionist behind the counter, he would immediately run up to some tree or plant they had in their lobby and begin sticking his fingers in the soil. He would then go into a little rant about how someone needed to water and feed the thing or it was going to die. Now they may not remember his name, but they sure wouldn't forget his face. He acted that way to stand out, but he also really felt bad for the plant.

A more appropriate (but not as memorable) example

might be the way you introduced yourself and certainly what you said when you left a lobby or someone's office. Acknowledge the gatekeeper because you will need his or her help some day with contact information or getting a message to someone important to you.

Clockwork

In my earliest years of selling, I can distinctly remember all the things I did during my sales calls and most of them were wrong—like talking too much and not getting enough of the potential customer's needs identified; and like not  tuning into the customer's personality and not picking up obvious clues. Yet, by many definitions, I was successful. How and why?

The reason is partially because these were the rules:

- I was expected to make 10 personal calls a day, five days a week.

- I was supposed to have three to four lunches per week at the hotel restaurant.

Having 50 plus personal meetings/sales calls per week makes for about 2,000 sales calls per year, which is a lot.

I would call on the same bigger potential clients once a week or once every few weeks until they booked. I thought I was a good salesperson, but the truth is they probably booked so I would stop coming by as often as I did. It was either that or they felt sorry for me. I'm convinced that even a bad sales call done enough times will produce positive results, but expect, train, and reinforce good sales calls and you and your team will obviously produce more.

I am also convinced that as we become more and more computer literate, we will become worse and worse at face-to-face meetings and eventually phone calls. There are many businesses where personalized service is expected, and this personal sales call, or service call will

make much more of an impression than an e-mail. I recently made about six e-mail inquiries to six different company Web sites about some work I wanted done that would approach $1 million a year for the company that was awarded the business. Out of the six, four did not respond. One sent an e-mail reply and one picked up the phone to call me. This is a million dollars people. Who is going to get that business? The company that makes a lasting positive impression and the one that truly cares and wants a relationship that earns loyalty will get the business. Can an e-mail or Web site produce those kinds of results? ■

Chapter XI: SMERFES

This is an acronym in the hotel world that stands for social, military, ethnic, religious, fraternal, education, and sports. It is the kind of business that has a higher probability of using hotel facilities during a lull, shoulder, or soft occupancy times—like holiday weeks, weekends, and slower months due to the climate (too hot, too cold or snow). As a trade-off for using hotels when business is needed the most, these groups look for greater value (lower pricing or better yet more inclusive benefits), and they know they can get it. After I talk about each of the letters in the acronym and provide tips on how to find and work with these groups, I'll share the most important lesson to be learned at the end of this section.

Social: Human resources departments of medium- to larger-sized companies are always having some sort of an affair that they need to plan—a retirement party, an anniversary of their company, a special event commemorating or launching something, holiday parties, etc.

Military: Military bases seem to have something going on at all times. For me, in the hotel world, it was something like a three- to four-day meeting to discuss some military minutia. In one assignment, I knew when the soldiers got paid, so we would market a getaway weekend for them and their buddies. Spouses, friends and family would also show up on these "payday" weekends and some would require overnight housing. It was very rare that they got out of control because they knew one phone call to the military commander was a fate worse than death.

Ethnic: Mexican, African American, Latin American or any kind of ethnicity will have some form of a club, association or group in every primary market and most secondary ones. I would meet with these groups and ask them what kinds of things they would do throughout the year that could or would involve the use of a hotel. When you combined all of the ethnic goings-on, it amounted to a return on investment worthy of my efforts.

Religious: Making sales calls to the churches, synagogues and mosques is very cool. They are nice to you, and just by their nature alone, they are very helpful—all around good people with which to talk and work. If that is not enough of an incentive to dig into this group of people, they also have business. We would hold weekend marriage retreats; have visiting speakers and musicians stay with us; be tuned into family reunions that were approaching; and much more. Rare is a place of worship that sits idle, so most have stuff going on quite frequently. There are major religious associations. One that comes to mind is the Religious Conference Managers Association that meets regularly to talk about best locations (and all which that entails) to hold conferences.

Fraternal: College fraternities—need I say more? There was this one particular marketing program I did that was especially successful. Most (not all) universities are looking for ways to fund their alumni association and the things they do as a group. We approached one particular national alumni group with the idea that if they gave a wallet-sized, laminated card telling about our hotel and its benefits to its members, we would donate a certain percentage of the room rate to the association each month. We said that very thing on the card in big print. The alumni handled getting the cards into the hands of their many thousands of members and the response was nothing short of terrific. In many cases, the alumni members would be traveling on business and would stay with us rather than their normal choice because of their loyalty to the alumni association. They did not care about spending more with us, as long as we made the donation. Along with the donation, the association members knew that we took good care of them while they stayed with us and that was all that mattered.

Education: I have spoken about this previously in different parts of this book, but high schools and colleges have all sorts of opportunities for those of us in the hospitality sector. Visiting sports teams, band camps, debate teams, visiting speakers, donors, continuing education events, parents' weekends, graduation and a long list of other events had an impact on my hotels.

Sports: This gets its own category because it has so much potential. We would work a relationship with parks and recreation departments funded by local cities and towns, and they would tell us what tournaments were being held in the area for many different age groups and sports. They would include our special offers on a fact sheet that they would send to all of their visiting team's coaches. Instead of waiting for coaches or team mangers to call us, we would call them in advance and create the right incentive for

them to use us and even promote us. If you don't have a parks and recreation in your immediate area, you will be surprised to know that there are still sports tournaments being held. Many times, in very large training events, I would role-play a phone call of a coach (me) calling my attendees' hotel. I would say to the front desk agent, "I am a coach of a girls' 12- year-old basketball team, and we have a tournament coming up over the July 4th weekend. I need to know what you charge for six rooms for five nights." I would then ask my audience what they heard and all too often they heard:

- I was a coach looking for a discount.

- I wanted my rooms located next to each other.

- I was coming during a time period for which they needed business badly.

- Some even heard that I was a coach who wanted to bring a bunch of brats to come steal their towels, and run up and down the hallways screaming all evening while leaving pizza boxes strewn throughout the hotel.

The truth is that both my kids played sports their entire lives, and the kids traveled so much that they were model guests. Sometimes the parents could be a handful, but this is easy to manage if you know how.

The real point I wanted to make was that the audience almost never heard the word tournament, which would lead them to think bigger than just six rooms for five nights. If they heard, thought, or sold the big picture, they would be filling up their hotel.

Amateur Athletic Union (AAU) is a very big sports organization that has teams in thousands of cities, towns and areas all across the United States. It comprises teams of boys and girls ages 7-18 who play basketball. High school coaches are not permitted to coach these teams, but they are often the catalysts for getting coaches to take the best talent from the area and play games all throughout the summer months to make their kids better prepared to compete when the school teams start playing again in the fall and winter. It is an absolute terrific opportunity for children to get in shape, stay in shape, and stay out of trouble. Kids develop basketball, team, and communication skills; learn how to win and lose; and much more about life's challenges. These teams play during holidays and many families make vacations out of these tournaments, so it is a financial boom to many hotels if they can capture this business.

Club soccer is much like the AAU example above. It is a very large body of teams that are very well organized. They play games or practice every day from when school closes until it re-opens.

Baseball and softball's elite teams are playing 60-70 games during the summer months in cities and towns in your area.

Football, swimming, lacrosse, volleyball, field hockey, and bowling could be in your area. For all of these sports, I would recommend you start by contacting the athletic director of your local high schools to find out who the AAU and similar coaches are from the school. From a meeting with these coaches, you can start to infiltrate the coaching network and realize a very healthy return on investment.

Don't forget about the cheerleading, pom-pom squads and dance teams. These groups often practice more, compete more, and certainly spend more on their "sport" than any others. Most high schools have a sponsor that can direct you to people with which you need to talk.

To reach these coaches and managers, you may have to call them at night. Now, none of us likes getting calls at home, but these coaches are used to it. If you are going to make their jobs easier, then they will welcome your phone call.

OK, I promised you a grand finale to this SMERFES section, so here it is.

At your main public library there are directories for clubs and associations that represent any and every kind of activity you could imagine. The National Association for the Mothers of Twins; National Tobacco Tin Can Club; The Guppy Club and National Association of Witches and Warlocks are just a sampling. This gives you a mental image of the different types of associations who meet and spend money to satisfy their interests.

I am certain that if you went online and did searches for these kinds of directories you would find more than enough to get you started on a quest to capture some of this business.

Keep in mind that most of these organizations are run by presidents who are elected each year. They are faced with getting up to speed in a hurry about how to plan and execute annual conferences. When my hotels called on these folks, we would impress upon them that we are experts who specialize in helping people just like them in order to make it easier for them to concentrate on other association business. We would take the worry out of their critically important event.

Because these presidents are not paid and have jobs during the day, we found that contacting them at night was the only way to communicate over the phone. While the competition's salespeople went home, we would conduct phone blitzes. I would bring in a few salespeople to stay until 9:30 p.m. making 50-75 prospecting phone calls. If they made 500 phone calls, we would realize 50 leads for our area and 20 would actually confirm meaning hundreds of thousands of dollars in

revenues for us. The best part was that this business would again be willing to meet at our hotel when we needed business the most—holiday weeks. I would set up a special incentive for the salespeople who made these calls. It was so special that they could pay for their holiday travel and gift buying from this one week of phone blitzing alone.

Chapter XII: Embarrassing Moments Do-Over

I don't think you can go on the offensive here, but you should be ready to help clients and potential clients with a do-over.

I worked in a hotel in the upper Midwest that was very reliant on airline crew business. So one of the very first things I did when I arrived as the new director of sales was to meet with all of the most important clients. I set up a meeting with a particular airline that was my second largest account in this office. I tried everything to make an emotional connection with this client, but being that he was extremely Stable/Analytic, it was very hard to get close. I left his office not feeling good about the meeting and not being able to create more loyalty. So in the many days and months ahead, I tried again and again to further solidify this relationship. The best I could get from him was that if he needed me, he would call. That wasn't good. My feeling was that this account was at risk to be stolen by my competition. If I was being paranoid and had no reason for concern, then fine. I just didn't want to think I had a loyal client only to have him stolen from me. It's better to be paranoid than victim to a theft.

Out of the blue, at the end of a day about a month after our last meeting, I am waltzing through the high-energy bar that we had on site and who do I spy sitting in a booth with a group of men and women who I assume to be airline folks? It was this client. I walked over and shook his hand and was introduced to the group. I asked if I could buy a round of drinks—an offer which he quietly but firmly turned down. Normally I would have just sent the waitress over with a tray of free drinks, but with him being so Stable/Analytic, I did not want to offend his sense of professional protocol.

Many hours later as the night progressed, I was surprised to see him still sitting there with a now smaller group from the original. It was clear that he had more than a few drinks. I nodded in his direction and he nodded back. It was not exactly an offer to come over and join him, so I left for the night.

The next morning he called me (the first time he initiated a call), so I cleared everything off the top of my desk and thought I was ready for anything.

On a side note, hoteliers have a high divorce rate. I was stupid enough at one time to think it was because of the incredibly long hours we worked and the few days we took off. Then someone further simplified it for me. A place with lots of beds plus a place that has lots of alcohol equals trouble for many. I was the guy too busy working.

Back to the airline contact who told me over the phone that he accidentally put his bar tab and a hotel room (said he didn't feel well and spent the night) on his personal American Express. Then he said he would like to come by the hotel and pay cash or use another card. Now I could be adding two plus two and coming up with five here, but it would only reason that he didn't want this bill to arrive in his mailbox where others could see it and come to accusatory conclusions. What would you do? I told him not to worry about the bill and that we would take care of it. He asked if I was sure. Of course I was.

He was no friendlier after that call, and I only saw him a few times during the year—when it was time to raise his rate and ask for his signature on the new agreement. But, I slept a little better at night with those incriminating photos that I had taken. I'm just kidding. This happened at a time before cell phones had built-in cameras. Besides, I don't even have a camera in my phone today, only because I feel I am too stupid to figure out how to work

it. Could you imagine what his reaction would have been to me asking the group to get together for a group photo? When presenting the photos, I could have said, "Here is one of the eight guys. And here's one at 2 a.m. when it's just the two of you. Wow, these are great photos, huh?"

There are all kinds of moral dynamics to consider. Did I condone this behavior? Did I make it make it easier for him to do it again, assuming that he did something wrong? I had come to grips with the fact that I was not his keeper. He made personal choices that I might not have made, but did that make him any worse than me? Let him cast the first stone. I had my hands full keeping me and my family straight, without policing others for whom I don't have direct responsibility for or influence over. If he would have asked my opinion, I would have been honest, but he didn't ask for my opinion.

Be the Decision Maker Your Clients Want and Need

How many situations have you encountered where you went against the direct orders of your boss and were ready to suffer the consequences, even if it meant your termination?

In this instance, I was already the director of sales of a hotel going through a major renovation when my fourth largest account transferred a new decision maker into our territory. It was a very frugal organization that would rather spend money on its employees' hotel stays than its own lobby furniture or offices. I visited the new arrival, and as we are wrapping up our getting-to-know-each-other meeting, I said that if there was ever anything he needed, including a favor, to call on me personally.

He half jokingly said that he could sure use some new furniture and asked if I had any contacts in the hotel business that could get him a good deal? I told him that I had some stuff he could have for free because we were renovating our lobby. It was good stuff, but not brand new. He was floored by my answer and asked when he could send his crew over to pick it up. I told him to give me a week, and I would have it delivered.

You are going to think I am making this up, but no sooner do I get back to my hotel and eye the lobby furniture that I was now planning to send over to my new contact, my general manager ran into me and said that he planned on putting the furniture in one of our suites. I tried my best to convince him that we needed new stuff in the suite, but he was adamant that it be the old lobby furniture. I am forced to come clean with my boss and tell him what I did and why. He was not fazed. In no way was I to touch that furniture. Once again, I was at a crossroads in my career.

I could have called up this new contact and told him that I goofed and that we could not send him what I thought we could, which is Portuguese for "I am a goober who makes promises I can't keep, so the next time I show up in your office to ask for your business, you should be too busy for me. In fact, you should find out who my boss is so that you talk with him and not me."

I may be a lot of things, but I'm no goober, so I made my decision. In about three days, I was going to be the manager on duty, which meant I not only did my "normal" job, but I was also the manager for the property until 11 p.m. Did I tell you divorce rates were high in the hotel business? Manager-on-duty time is prime time for doing what needed to be done.

The day before my manager-on-duty shift, I met with my maintenance chief who was responsible for the physical workings of the hotel and someone who was my equal on paper—both of us reported to the general manager. He could have told me to take a long walk off of a short pier after hearing my request, but he simply said, "So how many does this mean you will owe me?"

Friday night at 10 p.m., a mysterious van with my hotel's name on it showed up at the hotel's front door and several unknown men in hotel maintenance uniforms with nametags that I could not make out stole our lobby furniture. Later that night, two of those same gentlemen were seen drinking a 12-pack at the apartment of one of the maintenance men, but we didn't know who they were or who bought them the beer.

Amidst all the dirt and debris of the construction, it took the general manager a few days to figure out that our lobby furniture was even gone. Of course, when he came to me to find out if I knew what happened, all I could say was, "What are the odds that someone stole that stuff you were going to move into the suite?" People are so bold today. Don't you agree Mr. General Manager?" He was so busy with the construction project that he had little time to get upset at me because he was already upset about a few bigger hitches that he had to go fix. I escaped, and in hindsight, would do it all over again.

Here is another example of not wanting to lose face and trying to remain the decision maker that clients are desperate for today.

I'm now at a different hotel, and the largest client I ever had while working in a hotel, was coming over for lunch. This company had a policy of not accepting gifts—not even a free cup of coffee was allowed. The client made it clear, however, that gifts sent to her home were perfectly acceptable.

As she was joining me for the tasting of our new menu, she was complimenting our salt, pepper, and cheese shakers that were displayed all over the tables in our Italian restaurant.

It was time for me to transform from just Don, to "Don the Decision Maker" superhero. I told my waitress that I would like her to box up a new set of all three shakers and to give them to me before the end of the lunch. She retorted that they only had one set left. I told her that we were good because that set was mine.

Later we got up to go through the buffet line when at the center of the entire buffet is a lobster the size of a small German shepherd perched on top of the grand feast. My client couldn't help but comment on how huge the thing was and how she had never seen a lobster that large even though she was from the Boston area.

Yep, you guessed it. I asked my waitress to wrap up the "lobster dog." As the waitress began to object, I gave her a look that said, "I will have you cooked and put on top of tomorrow's buffet if you don't do what I ask." My client was beside herself with joy. She couldn't wait to show her husband.

Late that afternoon my counter-part in the food and beverage areas, and someone who owed me many favors, stormed into my office to find out where his pet lobster went. When I told him, he informed me that it took him a long time to find that lobster and he needed to charge me $500—what he claimed it cost him to buy it. We agreed on $100 that my department would pay.

Then he told me something that stopped me cold in my tracks.

It turned out that this lobster was meant only to be a decoration, a centerpiece, and it had been such a display for many months. I flashed to the vision of me attending the funeral of my biggest and best client because I poisoned her with this lobster that should not have been eaten. How do I tell her? She was so excited at the prospect of enjoying this feast over the weekend. It was now 4 p.m. on a Friday afternoon, so what should I do?

For once in my life, I was frozen with uncertainty. When I got around to calling her at the office, it was closed for the weekend. I'm doomed. The client was going to trace the food poisoning back to me, and while I did time, the account would leave and go elsewhere because I violated the company's no gift policy.

Monday morning she called me. As I answered the phone, I could feel my face all scrunched up dreading what she was going to tell me. It turned out that she was apologizing for messing up the lobster. She went on to say that she didn't know what she did wrong, but she was so sorry that she couldn't eat it. I in turn told her that the next time we got her a lobster that we would send our chef over to cook it for her. I apologized for not having thought of that sooner. Phew! She lived, and so did I, for another day. The moral of the story: Be the decision maker that makes fun, spur-of-the-moment decisions for your client, in front of your client so they know they are working with the right person. But by all means, make sure you don't give them stuff that could kill them.

Come See Us at Our Worst

Whenever I said, "Come see us at our worst" to a potential client, they would almost always ask me to repeat myself.

Fortunately, in most of the places I worked, our worst sleeping room was still something of which we could be proud. What if I said to the prospect that this room was equal to or better than the competition? I don't think that has the same impact as saying that this is the worst you will do, and it only gets better from here.

In the few places that I did have some not-so-great accommodations, I would not show those rooms, and I would not let my group get those rooms *unless* they had to be more rate-sensitive. I meant it when I said, "This is the worst you will do."

There was a chain of limited feature hotels based in the Midwest that I mentioned earlier in this book, which is worth repeating because it really relates to the notion of getting what you pay for—and hopefully more than that. This brand would build a room off of the lobby of its hotels and keep people from going in it by putting a red velvet rope across the doorway. When typical consumers would walk in without a reservation and want to see the room before they bought it, all the front desk agent would have to do is to tell them to take a look. I don't think they said this is the worst you will do, but I know they at least said, "Your room looks just like this one." I'd like to think that seeing stuff before you buy it is just part of the American way, or it ought to be.

My partner and I had a company for a few years that specialized in leasing apartment units. We would go into an apartment community and determine how many days it would take us to lease its current vacancies. Let's say it was 80 units in X amount of days. Then we would guarantee our client that the units would be leased to her specifications or we would not get paid. Nobody did it then, and I don't think anyone does that now. We would still be doing it except that we didn't enjoy working with the apartment ownership groups as much as we did the hotel owners. Anyway, my point is that we would tour the competition. There would be a good-looking, well-educated, good-smelling, professional leasing agent who showed us the units by saying

things like, "This is the kitchen. This is the closet. And here is the bedroom," as if we could not see this for ourselves.

We applied all of the techniques in this book and we made a great deal of money in the apartment world, but it is way behind the hospitality world when it comes to knowing how and where to sell.

You Big Dummies

I have to admit that I picked this idea up from the same client who I talked about in the Sex Sells section. The client had taken a real sleeping room and permanently placed very expensive mannequins in it. I guess good dummies cost a lot of money (human ones too).

They placed a man on the bed talking on the phone and put the woman at the desk working on a laptop computer.

When the client would bring prospective customers on a tour, he would ask them to enter the room first and the prospects would always jump up and back up once they saw that the room was occupied.

The salesperson, no matter how many times he had done this, would genuinely laugh at their reaction and ask them to go back in, which they would do very tentatively. The salesperson would then say to take a good look and the prospects would also enjoy a great laugh.

The client would then take the prospects into the bathroom and in a load of suds was a woman (sex sells). The salesperson would point out that his hotel wanted the guest to visualize how functional and comfortable the room was and this was the best way to show them.

This was a huge hit. No competitor would invest in taking a room out of inventory and then spend the money my client did on mannequins, not to mention the designer outfits they wore. I guess you could say this was another reason why he went bankrupt, but I would say that this "look at how you fit" idea is one that will set you apart in a big way.

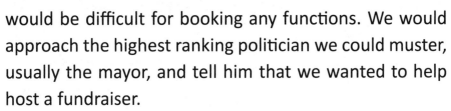

Politicians in Your Pocket

We would take a look at our calendar for the year and pick several dates that we knew would be difficult for booking any functions. We would approach the highest ranking politician we could muster, usually the mayor, and tell him that we wanted to help host a fundraiser.

We would tell the politician that our goal was to help him pull together the right people for their birthdays,

anniversaries, or some other landmark date that came close to our lull-period dates.

He could have the fundraiser be whatever fit his agenda. All we asked was to break even on the affair. He would take the money and spend it on a re-election campaign or give the money to a chosen charity.

We provided the space, the food and the bar, and the mayor's office did all the rest. They brought in high caliber people to attend with whom we did not have the credibility—not yet, anyway. It was an inexpensive way for us to have access to an audience we couldn't have reached on our own. They would then become prospective new clients. Here's wishing a happy birthday to you Mr. Mayor. ▪

Chapter XIII: Showing Your Competition How to Steal

You have businesses that you have booked in the past that no longer fit your needs—so much so that you are now losing revenues because they consume availability that could go to potentially higher paying customers. How do you tell your clients, who have been loyal to you, that you no longer value their business? It's a tough one.

This would typically happen to my hotels when we were forecasting a slow down for a long period consequently booking an account at a low room rate. That account would then use us on a transient basis. This might happen because of a recession; a new hotel opening in the area creating stagnant demand; your physical location was not in keeping with what the consumer wanted; or a combination of all of these issues.

Our team would address these issues by looking for replacement business for this older account. Some hotels would make rash decisions and fire the client (tell them they could not use the hotel anymore) without having secured new business first. They tried replacement when they should have been thinking displacement.

Our strategy was to tread lightly because we may need that client back someday if we run into another recession or that client's profile changed for the better. For example, the client merged with another company which increased its ability to pay more or do more. What about the decision maker leaving this company and running a different company in your market. How would she react when she found out her new company was using your product or service and you fired her in the past? That would not be good.

Instead, what we would do was to find a new piece of business first with the potential to use us more and pay us more, but we could not fit both into our hotel. We would identify which client had the least potential for us and we would accidentally tell our competition (usually over a beer) that we were going to have to raise the rates on this terrific account which had been with us for so long. We would not discuss rates. That is price fixing and highly illegal.

Sometimes my competition was so stupid that I would have to go on and tell them the name of the company because they did not know to ask. I would obviously be in the mood to talk, so I tried to make it easy for the competition to know all the necessary details.

I would then go to my old account contacts and tell them that we needed to raise their rates because of our demand and their new rates would be X. Once in a blue moon, they would agree to pay the new rate, but most often they would say that they could not or would not pay that much.

We would do this with a lot of empathy and a lot of regret (which was genuine because these folks helped us be successful), but realized it was a necessary business decision. The closest I could come with an analogy here is when a sports franchise trades an aging veteran away to a competitor. You understand why, but you still feel bad for all involved.

Hopefully our competitor would make a sales call "out of the blue" with competitive rates and secure this account. If they didn't I would have to assume that they were in a Chamber of Commerce meeting hunting for business or in a staff meeting that lasted a week. If that was the case we had to suggest to the client that they try Competitor Hotel (the one with which we had beer).

The competition can be stupid. I was going to say dummies, but not after that good dummy story you just read. The dummies deserve more credit than the competition sometimes.

After the recommendation, we would keep in touch with that old account which was with our competition. This relieved our conscience to a small degree; and we never knew if we would need them again someday.

I once had to go back to an account that I gave away. He asked me eye ball to eye ball, "Will you ask me to leave again someday if I come back to your hotel?" I told him the truth—it was a possibility. He was so taken aback by my honest answer that he returned.

Dead People Don't Know It's a Recession

When we lived in New York City, my father worked for a company that would buy up old precious metals and melt them down to make new jewelry and stuff. I would ask him what kinds of things he bought, and it was what you expected—things like silver service tea sets, souvenir spoons and even rags that precious metal milling machine workers would use to wipe off their machines. They would pay scrap metal prices which was a lot lower than what the markets were paying for raw bars.

One item they paid scrap prices for (which puzzled me at first) were teeth. He said people would bring in teeth filled with gold and gold amalgam. I asked if they bought from dentists, but he said most came from funeral homes. As a kid growing up in Brooklyn, you didn't have to tell me how funeral homes happened to find a few teeth laying around.

Subconsciously, I guess I never forgot that story of how funeral homes are really places of business like tire stores. Sure, the employees of funeral homes can have empathy, but after awhile you have to become immune to all the crying and grieving, and start counting dead bodies like you count cars coming in for new tires. They have seen and heard every emotion known to man. I think I would fall victim to those emotions too, but I'm certain to get a few letters on this next stealing technique.

When I started looking at any and all means of producing business for my hotels, I would look at the funeral home business as a terrific opportunity to pick up relatively last minute business at a generally higher rate. Because I knew the funeral directors were business men and women—some who would even stoop to pulling teeth for a few bucks—I decided to be right up front and treat them as I would a travel agent. I offered them 10 percent of the business they sent to me.

I did some consulting work for a hotel recently that was losing a lot of money. It needed to stop the bleeding immediately. One of the first things the hotel did was make sales calls to funeral homes in the area and the hotel booked $10,000 in the first two weeks.

So God bless the deceased, and God bless the funeral director who doesn't pull the poor deceased's teeth. Be sure these funeral directors understand that you know the right things to say and do for these emotionally charged families, and reward them for sending you the business.

Local Yokels

Don't forget that the people who live in your backyard are consumers too. We spend so much time, money and energy trying to get someone who lives a thousand miles away from us to hear about and buy our product or service, and we often forget about the people who live 30 feet away.

While I was working at my first airport-area hotel I developed a weekend package that was price/value driven. I counted on locals to take advantage of it as a "close" getaway. The hotel had a pool, Jacuzzi, sauna, and a great bar and restaurant. This was enough to get people excited, but I couldn't forget that the hotel was located two miles from the airport. That location came with the frequent jet noises and a lack of things to do in the immediate area. As a result, our team had to develop activities the guests could do inside the hotel.

On my first attempt, I developed a lower-rated offering and printed it on a four-color brochure for our three-star hotel. I sold very few, until I put that same package together using the same rates on a black and white "budget" looking flyer. I guess I concluded from this experience that the expensive looking brochure did not speak to my budget-conscious consumers.

The message was one suggesting that receivers of the flyer put those visiting relatives that would normally stay at their homes, at our hotel and all would be happier. We also suggested that they personally spend a weekend at our hotel to unwind and have some fun, without having to drive great distances or spend a lot of money.

Those local weekend guests also became our base for weddings, catered events, lounge business and meetings users. I don't think we would have gotten these folks to use our facilities unless we made it easy for them to stay on weekends.

Same goes for your restaurants and lounges. Get a local following going and this market will grow vertically and horizontally.

Van Tail

Following your competition's vans or trucks can tell you something about their customers. I know it works in hotels, but I am also thinking about delivery trucks, automobile dealer courtesy vans, and other businesses that drop off or pick up customers.

Follow the van or truck for a day or more and see what locations they are frequenting. Then call on those accounts and liberate them.

An Owner Rules

Having owners and managers making sales calls creates a huge impact. It amazes me how few owners and managers make sales calls, and the ones that do aren't making a big deal about telling the prospect who they are.

Potential and existing clients like knowing that the top dog is interested in them and that they are important enough for this leader to visit with them.

Your position as owner isn't something you brag about. Keep your ego in check. You just need a humble  mention that you are the owner or the manager, and you like to meet with your best accounts or newest accounts— whatever it is you are doing.

I've been on many sales calls where the owner or manager didn't have a clue on how to make a sales call, but he didn't have to. All he had to say was that he was the owner and he was there to find out what it took to get the business.

The potential clients would usually just start pouring out details.

How many of your competitors' owners and top managers make sales calls? Regardless of that answer, you need to make these calls if you want to increase sales.

What message does it send to your employees when they see the owner or manager making calls? How does that impact your culture? Your employees will take on your personality and work habits, and chances are, they won't even know it. So, you can stay in that office and make paperwork, computer work, and meetings your top priority, or you can get out and grow your sales.

Get Back in Your Cubicle

I love this story. It is not my story but one that was told to me, and I think it's worth repeating for you.

There was this gentleman who worked for a convention and visitors bureau in a U.S. naval shipyard city. His job was to do market research for the sales office, which meant he was

expected to go through stacks and stacks of magazines and books looking for leads.

He would find what he thought would be a lead and qualify it for the proper salesperson. All the salesperson had to do then was to call the warm prospects and convince them that his city should host their upcoming conventions.

As he was studying the research materials, he saw a lot of naval reunions that were being planned. Without having a salesperson dedicated to that market, the researcher brought this information to the attention of the convention and visitors bureau director.

The director, of course, did what too many leaders do when a pot scrubber, shoeshine man, or in this case, a low-ranking research person comes to them with a good idea. He dismissed it, and told our hero to go back to his hollowed-out closet, turned office, and get back to researching.

Not one to let a good idea die, our hero typed up a simple, 20-page black and white booklet and advertised this "How to Plan a Military Reunion" book in one of the trade publications that he used for research.

The initial 100 sold out quickly, so he printed up some more. And those sold out. Pretty soon, this how-to book was in demand, and the researcher became known as an expert that could teach these many incoming presidents of the military reunions how to plan and execute their most important function for the year.

Our hero went on to start his own military reunion business. It got to be so large that he and his staff occupied three offices at a hotel in their downtown area for free because he could bring in so much business. Today his company is doing over $500,000 a year in revenues with a staff of 10 planning all types of military reunions.

Why do I love that story? There are many reasons, but for starters, it is an example of why bosses need to listen to everyone on their staff. Employees have good ideas.

For example, you would likely go to the customer first in a restaurant to find out what is good on the menu and what is not good, but who is the second person you would ask? Perhaps it is the waitress or waiter. My second choice would be the dishwasher. Why? He or she is the one who throws the food away. When is the last time someone asked a dishwasher what their customers liked or did not like? ■

Conclusion

I get to attend a lot of conferences and read a lot of books on my many travels. I see a lot of speakers and authors spending time and energies on attempting to motivate their listeners to do something. That's fine for some, but for many in the audience I feel that they are already motivated, they just need to know how to perform certain skills or learn how to do certain things. That's who I wrote this book for, people wanting to learn about skills and how to go about improving themselves and the situation for their families, their employees and themselves.

I hope you found this book to be more tactical and practical at showing you how to steal business that belongs with you and not the competition. They don't deserve that business because you will care more and do more for that account than your competition will. If you don't, you too will lose the business and your good employees will also soon follow.

In this book you read that if businesses did a better job of stealing business then we as consumers would be getting better service, not the continually and progressive worse that we are experiencing. Technology is supposed to make service providing better? Technology is a good thing but if it does not help people to be better service providers then those technology providers will be looking to cut people out of the service providing equation. That will be a very sad day.

If you knew someone was going to be able to steal your business because you did not make that account or your employees loyal, believe me, you would work harder and smarter to hang onto them. As it is today businesses don't know enough about how to steal and certainly don't know enough about how to make accounts loyal. That can all change for you because this book was written so that you could do both steal and make people more loyal.

So as you go about in life getting crappy service from people and companies you buy stuff from, half of you will be delighted. Your local AutoZone store (remember I said that I have an issue with you and I live only 1 mile from your world headquarters), to your local McDonalds to the cable company and your local energy provider service is not getting better.... it is getting worse. You will be delighted because you know how to deliver loyal and you know how to steal ethically and lawfully. You are about to become very rich in the process. Happy stealing people. ■

Acknowledgements

Thanks to Dr. Rick Johnson for his veteran book writing tips.

Thanks to Dr. Nate Booth for his direction.

Thanks to Barb Michlitsch who helped with transcribing and who more importantly also prays for me for all the bad stuff I've done.   And will do.

Thanks to Amanda Gambill for her great editing.

Thanks to my talented sister, Patti Farrell, for her great cover and manuscript design work, and all the other incredible work she does for me.

Thanks to Erin Wyles for showing me how to market the book using the latest social channels. And then showing me again and again.

Thanks to the following folks I bounced ideas off of and who helped me rekindle some of my old tricks and pick up a few new ones: Peter Smith, George VonAllmen, Scott Schilling, Greg Asvestas, Dennis Noonan and Craig Poole.

Editor
Amanda Gambill

Amanda began working for my training company in 2004 as a part-time newsletter editor. She therefore said she really couldn't turn me down when I asked her to edit her first book.

She has been writing and editing professionally for more than 10 years, typically in a marketing and communications capacity. Amanda has also been a freelance writer for nearly 10 years.

When you hire Amanda for your writing and editing needs, you will get a passion for doing things creatively and correctly combined with a collaborative spirit.

Connect with Amanda on LinkedIn or e-mail her directly at ceoqueen1213@yahoo.com.

Don Farrell

Contact Information

Don@FreshRevenues.com

www.FreshRevenues.com

731-514-1589

Other Don Farrell Books in the Works

Small Business Bible—How to Make Your Business Successful

Making FRESH Money Tonight—Converting Inquiries

Why Your Employees Hate You

How to Distance Yourself from Your Competition Once and For All

How to Start Your Own Company

A Life in the Day of Kid's Play... How not to screw up your kids

How People Really Learn—Training Anybody and Everybody

Training Doesn't Work ... Unless You Do It This Way

All I Want To Do Is Fix One Airline

To pre-order one of these books at a considerable savings, visit www.FreshRevenues.com.